WEREWOLVES

WERE-WOLVES
BY JIM HASKINS

FRANKLIN WATTS
New York/London/Toronto/Sydney
1981

Frontispiece:
Lon Chaney, Jr.,
in The Wolfman (1941).

Photographs courtesy of
Movie Star News: pp. ii, 46, 76, 84, 98;
New York Public Library Picture Collection:
pp. 5, 32, 39, 62;
Animals Animals/M. A. Chapell: p. 8
Animals Animals/M. Stouffer: p. 12

Library of Congress Cataloging in Publication Data

Haskins, James, 1941–
Werewolves.

Bibliography: p.
Includes index.
Summary: Discusses werewolf legends
of different countries, actual cases of werewolves,
ways to protect oneself against these creatures,
and how to cure an afflicted person.
1. Werewolves—Juvenile literature.
[1. Werewolves] I. Title.
GR830.W4H37   398.2'454   81-3338
ISBN 0-531-04323-1   AACR2

Copyright © 1981 by James S. Haskins
All rights reserved
Printed in the United States of America
5 4 3 2 1

CONTENTS

CHAPTER I
What Is a Werewolf?
1

CHAPTER II
How the Wolf Got Such a Bad Reputation
7

CHAPTER III
How the Werewolf Myth Got Started
14

CHAPTER IV
*Mental and Physical Diseases
That Added to the Werewolf Myth*
20

CHAPTER V
Not All Werewolves Were Bad
25

CHAPTER VI
But Most Were Terrible
29

CHAPTER VII
Werewolf Stories from Britain
34

CHAPTER VIII
Werewolf Stories from Scandinavia
37

CHAPTER IX
Werewolf Stories from Poland
41

CHAPTER X
Werewolf Stories from
Other
East European Countries
45

CHAPTER XI
Werewolf Stories from Italy
49

CHAPTER XII
Werewolf Stories from Germany
52

CHAPTER XIII
Werewolf Stories from France
57

CHAPTER XIV
Persecution of Werewolves
61

CHAPTER XV
The Case of Peter Stump
67

CHAPTER XVI
Three Werewolf Cases in France
70

CHAPTER XVII
How to Become a Werewolf
74

CHAPTER XVIII
How to Spot a Werewolf
82

CHAPTER XIX
Protection Against Werewolves
87

CHAPTER XX
How to Kill a Werewolf
92

CHAPTER XXI
How to Cure a Werewolf
96

CHAPTER XXII
The Myths Persist
105

Some Other Books About Werewolves
111

Index
113

WEREWOLVES

CHAPTER I
WHAT IS A WEREWOLF?

A werewolf, as anyone who has ever seen a werewolf movie knows, is a wolf-man (or a wolf-woman). It is a human being who assumes the apparent form of a wolf at night and then goes around attacking and eating other animals and sometimes even people.

The term comes from an old English word, or combination of words. *Wer* means man, so a wer-wolf is a man-wolf. Nowadays, we usually spell it *werewolf*, but you can still find writers about witchcraft who like the old spelling *werwolf* better.

The werewolf is just one of many man-animals that human beings have envisioned or believed in throughout history. How about in those parts of the world where there have never been any wolves? Instead of werewolves, the people in these parts have believed in other man-monsters. In India, people believed in were-tigers; in various parts of Africa there have been beliefs in were-leopards, were-jaguars, were-hyenas, were-lions, were-elephants, were-crocodiles, were-alligators, and even were-sharks. In Latin America, people have believed in were-jaguars, were-eagles, and were-serpents; in China, were-tigers, were-foxes, and were-cats were the favorites.

Some Indian tribes in North America have believed not only in werewolves but also in were-buffalo. In fact, no matter where they have lived, people have always believed in the ability of some individuals to change their form from human to animal.

Depending on the culture and the time in history, people with the power to change their form in this way were thought to be either lucky or unlucky, helpful or evil. In Africa and Latin America the power was seen as a gift from some god or spirit, given to the human being for the purpose of revenge. People who had been hurt as humans could turn into wereleopards or were-jaguars and attack those who had done them harm. They also sometimes used their powers to help other people. Even werewolves are said to have been looked upon more kindly in ancient times. But after the birth of Christianity, the attitude toward werewolves changed in most places. For hundreds and hundreds of years the werewolf has been thought of almost completely as an evil monster.

Werewolves and vampires are often linked together in legend, but they are really quite different. A werewolf is a living creature; it has not returned from the dead, like a vampire. In fact, many people believed that when a werewolf died, it returned to earth as a vampire. In old stories and legends you will sometimes hear about people who have died and returned to earth as werewolves. The people of Serbia use the same word, *voukodlak*, to describe both vampires and werewolves. But there are not many stories about werewolves turning into vampires. Whether the legends come down to us from France, Germany, or Hungary, from five hundred years ago or fifty years ago, they usually talk about werewolves as living creatures, like witches.

Also like witches, werewolves are usually thought to like being man-animals. There have always been stories about unfortunate people who became werewolves by accident of birth or because some wicked person put a spell on them or because they were careless about where they slept when the moon was full. But there are more stories about people who willingly change into beasts. In animal form they can kill animals and people and satisfy their hunger for raw flesh. Then they can change back into human form and not get caught.

That's why Peter Stump, or Stubb, said he became a werewolf. He was executed for being a werewolf in Germany in the 1500s. Before he died, he freely confessed to all his crimes and explained that he would turn himself into a wolf in order to take out "his malice on men, women, and children, in the shape of some beast, whereby he might live without dread of danger of life, and unknown to be the executor of any bloody enterprise which he meant to commit."

This is quite a different story from the ones told in modern werewolf films. In most of these films, the werewolf cannot help himself. He turns into a werewolf without wanting to. Actually, the way we think of the werewolf today is different in several ways from the way people thought of werewolves a few hundred years ago.

Another difference is that we usually think of werewolves as men. But throughout history people have thought that women could be werewolves, too. Plenty of women as well as men were arrested and executed as werewolves in Europe in the 1500s. One of the most celebrated werewolf cases in history involved a woman. Elizabeth Bathory, of a noble family in Hungary, was said to have changed herself into a wolf and killed more than six hundred virgins in order to renew her youth by bathing in their blood. Caught and convicted of werewolfism in 1610, she died in prison in 1614.

Earlier in this century, people still thought of werewolves as both men and women. The first film ever made about werewolves (*The Werewolf*, 1913) was about an Indian wolf-girl. In 1946, *She-Wolf of London* was made by an American filmmaker. But the majority of films, and especially the recent ones, have been about wolf-men.

Probably the biggest difference between how we think of werewolves and how our ancestors thought about them is that we don't believe in them. At least most of us don't. Four hundred years ago, most people did believe in werewolves. The monsters were hated and feared, and there were all sorts

Women rarely captured
werewolf roles in film.
Nina Foch, in Cry of the Werewolf
(1944), was an exception.

of prescriptions about how to recognize them, protect yourself from them, and kill them. It may be hard for us in modern times to understand this fear of werewolves on the part of people who lived hundreds of years ago, but it shouldn't be so hard for us to understand how the fear got started. The fear of werewolves began because of fear of the wolf.

People are still afraid of wolves. They would fear wolves even more if there were more wolves around to be afraid of. But there are not many wolves around anymore. In fact, the animal is practically extinct. Although it has a wider range than any other mammal and can live in forests or plains, mountains or lowlands, cold climate or warm, the wolf is a striking example of what happens to an animal under great persecution. No other animal has been more hated or feared by humans.

CHAPTER II
HOW THE WOLF GOT SUCH A BAD REPUTATION

Now that the wolf is in danger of extinction in most parts of the world, some people are saying that it doesn't deserve its bad reputation. These people want to preserve the earth's ecology, and they do not want any more animals to become extinct. So they are trying to get the public to care about what happens to the wolf. They say that wolves are afraid of people and are not likely to attack them. And this is generally true of the wolves that have managed to survive. Hundreds of years ago, however, when there were many wolves, they were not so afraid of humans. And they were not at all afraid of the animals that humans kept for food.

It is probably the liking for human livestock that first caused the wolf to be hated by people. Wolves have killed sheep and goats ever since people started raising these animals. In Northern Europe a murderer or a thief was called a wolf, and a wolf that was captured was hanged right along with thieves and robbers. The old Saxon name for the gallows means "wolf-tree."

The way wolves behave does not help their reputation.

They tend to travel in packs and to hunt at night. They are stealthy and silent. They usually catch the animals that are the easiest prey—the old, the very young, or the injured. They are gorgers and will eat every part of an animal but the bones. All these qualities make the wolf even more hated than other animals of prey. They also cause the wolf to be more feared.

There is something eerie, almost supernatural, about the wolf. In early English use, the word *wolf* was used to describe the devil. Ancient Etruscan vases have been dug up that show Charon, the man who pilots the ferryboat that carries souls to hell, wrapped in a wolf's fur. The wolf became a symbol of bad luck and disappointment—a symbol of night and winter, storm and death.

Only rarely has the wolf ever been considered lucky. Pliny, an ancient Roman historian, wrote that it was good luck if a wolf crossed your path and turned to its right; it was especially good luck if the wolf's mouth was full. Pliny also wrote of the ancient belief that there is a special hair in a wolf's tail that, if a person were brave enough to snatch it from a live wolf, could be used to induce love. In Sicily, it is a traditional belief that a person who wears a wolf's skin will be very brave and that a wolf's foot will protect against a variety of pains.

Italian country folk in the late 1500s put a wolf's head with wide gaping jaws over the doors of their huts to defend against sorcerers and witches. They also believed that eating roast wolf would make them immune from evil spells.

In ancient Ireland, wolves' teeth set in silver were carried as good-luck charms. But mostly, the wolf was thought to be evil and bad luck.

From ancient times the wolf has been a common villain in stories and legends. Ancient Greek proverbs depict the wolf as a dangerous and treacherous beast. He was a "stock villain" in Aesop's fables, written around 570 B.C. In no less than thirty-seven of these fables, the wolf is the chief character.

In *The Shepherd and the Wolf*, for instance, the wolf gains the shepherd's confidence, talks him into leaving the flock in his care, and then promptly destroys all the sheep.

In *The Wolf and the Crane,* the wolf has a bone stuck in its throat. The long-billed crane reaches in and pulls it out. But when the crane asks for a reward, the wolf says she has reward enough in getting her head safely out of his mouth.

Even the Bible talks about the wolf as an untrustworthy character. Matthew says, "Beware of false prophets, who come to you in clothing of sheep, but inwardly they are ravening wolves." We still have a saying that is much like Matthew's warning: Beware of the wolf in sheep's clothing.

Many popular fairy tales that have come to us from Europe have wolf villains. *The Three Little Pigs* and *Little Red Riding Hood* are two of them.

The quote from Matthew in the Bible is just one saying about wolves that has come down to us through the years. For example, when people say they are managing to get by on what they have, or are staying out of debt, they might say they are keeping the wolves from the door. That saying comes from an ancient Greek proverb.

When a woman says a man is a wolf, she means that he is too fast or comes on too strong. The idea is that the man is like a wolf attacking an innocent sheep.

Some people still say that if you are very hungry you "have a wolf in your stomach."

When someone eats too fast, we say he or she "wolfs down" food.

And how about "crying wolf"? That means to raise a false alarm.

You can get a pretty good idea from these sayings how hated and feared the wolf used to be. It attacked weaker animals. It always seemed to be hungry and ate ravenously when it got food. People were so afraid of it that they would sometimes think they saw it even when it wasn't there.

Add to all this some other wolf characteristics, and the fears become even easier to understand. Wolves howl in the night and bay at the full moon. They have slanted eyes that glow yellowish-green in the moonlight and red in firelight. And they have been known to attack human beings; there are many stories of such attacks in history.

The wolf is a fierce enemy and has many traits that disgust humans.

In ancient Britain, tribes trying to settle amidst the huge forests on the island came up against savage packs of wolves that did not know about humans and so were not afraid of them.

In the 900s, a king of the Saxon tribe in Europe built what was called a "hospital for the defense of way-faring people passing that way from Wolves, lest they should be devoured."

In 1603, in the Gascony region of France, wolves began to attack children and even adults in broad daylight. And as recently as a century ago in some isolated parts of Russia, savage wolves were attacking people. In one year there were reports of 161 people being killed by wolves.

But people have had their revenge. Wolf hunting used to be a favorite sport in Europe. The Irish wolfhound was bred just for tracking wolves. Sometimes, local authorities would pay bonuses to hunters for every wolf pelt they brought in.

People still hunt wolves in areas where there are any wolves left to hunt. Until very recently the wolf was hunted in Sweden by people in helicopters and snow scooters. Then around 1972, it was discovered that there were only about forty wolves left in the whole country.

Small numbers of wild wolves continue to survive in parts of Scandinavia, Finland, Italy and Sicily, Yugoslavia, Albania, and Bulgaria. More are to be found in North America, especially Alaska, and in Asia and Eurasia. But the wolf may never again be an important member of the animal world. Like many other wild animals, it has been a victim of an increasing world population and fast-disappearing wilderness zones. It has also been the victim of a centuries-old hatred by humans.

CHAPTER III
HOW THE WEREWOLF MYTH GOT STARTED

A combination of fiction and fact led to the belief in werewolves. In the last chapter we talked about how much the wolf was hated and feared. We also talked earlier about how people in just about every culture have believed that human beings can change into animals. There is a very definite mythical source for the European belief in werewolves. It comes from Greece.

The ancient Greeks believed in many gods. Zeus was the most powerful of all. Hera, his wife, was called "mother of the gods." The Greeks believed that the gods had a great deal of contact with humans. Unlike the Christian, Jewish, or Moslem God, these gods would often come down from their home on Mt. Olympus to help or harm people. There were many legends about what they did for or against the Greek people.

In one legend, a man went too far in worshiping Zeus. He sacrificed a human child in the god's name. Some Greek writers made the story even more horrible by saying that the man then ate the child. The angry Zeus turned the man into a wolf. Naturally, since the myth was about a man turned into a wolf, the man was given the name Lycaon, from the Greek word *lykoi*, which means wolf.

After Lycaon's time, according to later Greek writers, similar transformations from man into wolf continued to occur quite often on the very same spot where Lycaon's shape had been changed. According to one legend, at certain times a member of the race of Anthos (probably a family of priests) was chosen to become a wolf. Men would draw lots, and whoever was chosen by lot would be taken to a lake in Arcadia where he would strip naked and hang up his clothes on an oak tree. Then he would swim across the lake and be changed into a wolf. For the next nine years he would roam with a pack of wolves through the wilderness. If, during those nine years, he had not tasted human flesh, he would be able at the end of that time to swim back across the river, put on his clothes, and go back to being a human again. But if he had tasted human flesh, he was doomed to wolfhood forever.

Also in Arcadia in ancient Greece, a group of people started worshiping a new god called Zeus Lycaeus. They named a nearby mountain Mt. Lycaeus (now Mt. St. Elias), and once a year they dressed in wolf masks and went to the mountain and had a feast that included animal and human meat mixed together. According to legend, whoever ate this mixture became a wolf and could not turn back into a man unless he ate no more human flesh for nine years.

Another group of ancient Greeks, the wild Maenad tribe, were also said to have worn wolf masks and to have had feasts of animal and human flesh. They would run after and catch an animal (or sometimes a man) and tear it to pieces. It is said that the Maenads were women, devotees of the god Dionysius.

The Romans, too, had their werewolf stories. One of the most famous comes from Rome in the first century A.D. It is not a myth like the myth of Lycaon, but a fictional story.

A man named Trimalchio decided to visit his girl friend one night and asked a friend to go part way with him. As they passed a cemetery, Trimalchio was amazed to see his friend stop, take off his clothes, and put them in a heap on the ground. He then urinated in a circle around them and turned into a wolf. Howling, he raced off into the woods.

Trimalchio tried to take up the clothes, but they had turned into stone.

Trimalchio rushed to his girl friend's house. When she saw him, she said, "Had you only come sooner you might have helped us, for a wolf broke in and worried our cattle. But he got the worst of it, although he escaped; for our hired man ran a spear through his neck."

Trimalchio had an idea that the wolf was his friend. He returned to the spot where the clothes were. They were gone, but the ground was covered with blood. At home, he found his friend being treated by a doctor for a bad neck wound.

"Then I knew he was a werewolf," Trimalchio said, "and after that I could never eat with him again, no, not if you had killed me."

Several parts of this early Roman tale crop up again and again in the folklore on werewolves—the change from man to wolf takes place at night, the man takes off all his clothes, a circle is created, and if the creature is wounded in wolf form it will have that same wound as a man.

In other parts of Europe there were wild tribes in ancient times whose customs and actions could have added to the wolf-man myth. These tribes came from northern Europe, where it was cold and where the people dressed in furs. Southern Europeans who were attacked by these tribes passed on to future generations tales of men dressed to look like animals. The scariest stories were about a Nordic tribe called *berserkers* who fought like wild men. The word *berserk* meant bearshirt in Norse. In the course of constant retelling of the story over the years, it was natural for the bearskin to become a wolfskin. The word *berserk* has come to mean hysterical or mad in our present-day language.

It is not necessary to go back to ancient times to find societies of animal-men. In Morocco in about 1465, the Isawiyya brotherhood was founded, and it still exists today in some areas of the African continent. Men would put on the furs of wolves, cats, lions, and hyenas (in later times they were more likely to wear garments painted to look like the skins of these animals), and they would dance around until they had worked themselves up into a frenzy. Then they would go on a "hunt" after young goats and sheep that they would catch and tear up with their bare hands and eat the meat raw. In some ceremonies these kids and lambs would be dressed in the clothing of women, clearly to act as substitutes for human victims.

There must have been many such tribes and societies in history. Otherwise, there could not have been so many tribal names that meant "wolf-men" or "she-wolf people" in Italy, Greece, Germany, and the Middle East. There were tribes called the Luvians, Luvanians, Dacians, and Hyrcanians— and all these names come from words meaning wolf.

In fact, there are a lot of names even today that mean wolf in other languages, not to mention the names that have *wolf* in them. Wolf and Wolfgang are common first names in Germany. The name Adolf comes from the Gothic words meaning "wolf of the land"; knowing that, you might decide Adolf Hitler was well-named.

Of course you can be named Adolf or Wolfgang, or you can have Wolf as your last name, and be proud of it. Having either a first or a last name that means wolf only points to a long history of interest in wolves on the part of people. Maybe one of your ancestors wore a wolfskin or was a brave killer of wolves. All our names have historical meaning or significance.

Although this book will concentrate on the werewolf legend in Europe, it is not necessary, as we have already seen, to look just at the folklore of Europe to find werewolf beliefs. There are several werewolf stories in Chinese folklore, for example. In one, a woodcutter is attacked by a big wolf in the woods one evening. The woodcutter climbs a tree and strikes at the wolf with his axe, cutting the animal's forehead. The wolf falls down and remains lying on the ground until dawn. Then he disappears. In the morning the woodcutter and his sons track the wolf to the hut of a peasant who has a cut on his forehead. The woodcutter's sons kill the peasant, and as he dies he changes into a wolf.

In another Chinese story a twenty-year-old youth becomes ill and loses weight because he sends out his soul in the shape of a wolf, killing and eating children every night. His father kills him, and as he dies he is transformed into a wolf.

There are also she-wolves in Chinese folklore. In the 800s, the mother of General Wang-hau of Tayuan in Shansi Province was said to have become a werewolf at the age of seventy. One night the servants saw a she-wolf come out of her bedroom and return to her room in the morning. Her husband was told, and he ordered her bedroom door locked and guarded. But the woman broke out through the trellis of a window and disappeared.

These stories certainly did not come out of an ancient Greek myth. But as you will see, they are very similar to European werewolf stories. Eastern werewolf beliefs arose out of people's fear and hatred of the wolf, just as Western werewolf beliefs did. And as we will see in the next chapter, there are some actual diseases that probably also contributed to the belief in werewolves.

CHAPTER IV
MENTAL AND PHYSICAL DISEASES THAT ADDED TO THE WEREWOLF MYTH

There is an actual mental disease in which the sufferer is under the delusion that he or she is a wolf or some other animal. Its name, *lycanthropy*, comes from the Greek words *lykoi* (wolf) and *anthropos* (man). People who suffer from this mental disease really believe they turn into wolves or other animals.

In the 1850s, a French doctor named Morel wrote about a man he treated for this mental disease. The man looked just like a man, but he was certain he looked like a wolf. Whenever people told him he didn't look like a wolf, he would argue with them. He would show his teeth and say they were fangs. He would show his feet and say they were paws. He would hold out his arm and point to imaginary long hairs on it. Nothing anybody could say could convince him that he was just imagining it all. He hated himself and begged to be shot.

Dr. Morel thought he might be able to help the man if he could make him see that he was not as cruel as a wolf. So, when the man was in a quiet mood, the doctor would bring children to see him. The man would take the children on his lap and be very gentle with them. But afterward he would hate himself even more. He felt he had somehow tainted them by hugging them.

The man finally died in an insane asylum, believing to the end that he was guilty of all sorts of crimes he could not possibly have committed.

Usually, people who suffer from this disease think that when they turn into animals they grow hair *on* their bodies. But once in a while there will be a person who suffers from this disease who thinks the hair grows on the *inside* of his or her body.

That was what a poor man in Italy believed in 1541. This man was convinced that he was a wolf, and he attacked and killed several people in the fields. The men of the town went after him and caught him. He looked quite human to them. But he kept insisting he was really a wolf. The only difference between himself and a wolf, he said, was that while wolves were hairy on the outside, his fur grew inside his body. His captors decided to check out his statement. They made deep cuts into his arms and legs and found no fur inside. Although he was treated by doctors, the man died of these wounds a few days later.

In the late 1600s in Russia, a man was brought before a duke in Moscow whose cattle he was accused of attacking and eating. The man was deformed and terrible to look at. His face and legs were covered with wounds, and he said he had been bitten by dogs while in the shape of a wolf. He told the duke that at Christmastime and at the time of the Feast of St. John the Baptist (in midsummer), a strange feeling would come over him. Hairs would sprout all over his body, and he would change into a wolf. The duke decided to test the man's story and ordered him locked up for over a year. During this time, both Christmas and St. John's Day came and went, and the man did not change shape. He was clearly a victim of the disease of lycanthropy.

There are also rare physical diseases that might have aided the werewolf myth. One is called *porphyria*. Its cause and cure are not known, but it seems to run in families. Something produced in the body causes hair to grow on normally bare skin. Sometimes the skin becomes yellowish in color. There can also be sores on the skin that break open. The teeth may turn reddish. In later stages of the disease, daylight hurts the eyes, and the victim acts wildly.

Another rare physical disease is *hypertrichosis*, which basically means overproduction of hair. It is another disease that is passed down from parent to child. People who have it get long, silky hair all over their bodies except on the palms of their hands, the soles of their feet, the ends of their fingers and toes, and their lips. Often they are missing their back teeth, so they have to chew everything with their front teeth. That causes them to gnaw a lot and look like dogs when they are eating.

A very famous case of this disease was recorded in the 1500s. Peter Gonzales, born in 1556 in the Canary Islands, had long dark hair all over his body. There was so much hair on his face that it is said he couldn't see unless his hair was curled up and out of his eyes.

In those days many kings in Europe collected strange-looking people. Just about every court had its resident dwarf. Henry II of France heard about Peter Gonzales and sent for him. The king was very pleased to find that Peter was quite intelligent, and he hired a tutor for him. The king enjoyed Peter's company, for the hairy young man was very witty. Peter was given anything he desired and was allowed to marry a normal girl. The king sent them on a tour of Europe for their honeymoon. He even trusted and respected Peter enough to give him messages to take to the other crowned heads of Europe.

It is not known how many children Peter and his wife had, but at least three of them inherited the disease from him. At least one of those three passed it on to the next generation.

Dr. Robert Eisler, author of the book *Man into Wolf*, stated in it that he had a friend whose head and neck showed normal hair growth but that the rest of his body was covered with hair as thick and black as the pelt of a bear. Even the upper parts of his feet were thickly covered with hair. The man was very gentle but also brave, and he won a medal as an Austrian infantry captain in World War I.

Diseases like these do not strike very often, but there can be little doubt that the rare cases that have occurred in history helped to further the werewolf myth long ago.

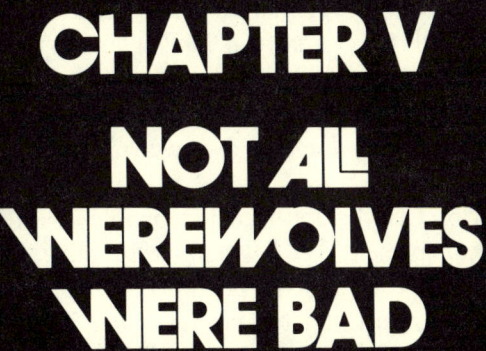

CHAPTER V
NOT ALL WEREWOLVES WERE BAD

In ancient folklore, werewolves were sometimes portrayed as kindly or helpful. A few tales of good werewolves have come down to us from later history as well. There are stories about swimmers saved from drowning by werewolves. There are tales about werewolves bringing food to starving travelers. There are even legends about werewolves protecting priests from wild animal attacks.

Ireland has one of the strongest traditions in this respect. Early English travelers in Ireland reported that the Irish took wolves as godfathers, prayed to them, and used their teeth as charms. (Ireland was known in England up to the end of the 1700s as "The Wolfland," and there is a well-known breed of dog called the Irish wolfhound that was originally bred as an especially large and powerful greyhound to hunt fierce wolf packs.)

It is part of Irish legend that the people of a district called Ossory (near present-day Ulster) were once cursed by an abbot. Ever since then, two people at a time were changed into werewolves and had to stay that way for seven years. If they had managed to survive after the seven years were up, those two would be free of the curse. But two more people would have to take their place. The following is an Irish tale about one of these unfortunate couples.

A priest and a young boy were journeying from Ulster to Meath. One evening, while they were sitting by a fire they had built in the woods, a wolf suddenly appeared. It saw that they were frightened and told them in a human voice not to be afraid.

The wolf explained that he was from Ossory, and that he and his wife had been forced to turn into werewolves because of the abbot's curse. His wife was ill and near death, and he asked the priest to go to her. Still trembling with fear, the priest followed the wolf to a tree not far away. In the hollow of the tree lay a female wolf. She thanked the priest for coming and begged him to give her Communion.

The priest was not sure if he should administer this holy sacrament to a wolf, even if the wolf sounded like a person. The male wolf persuaded the priest to do so when he pulled the female wolf's hide back to reveal the body of an old woman.

The priest gave the woman Communion, and the husband replaced the pelt over his wife. Then the wolf-man returned with the priest to the campsite. The next morning, he pointed out the best and shortest way for the two travelers to take as they continued on their journey. He thanked the priest again and promised that if he lived out the period of the curse (two-thirds of it had already passed) he would do more to show his gratitude. Then he disappeared into the forest.

One werewolf tradition in Portugal holds that the person who turns into a wolf is under an evil curse and is to be pitied, for this type of werewolf is a very timid creature.

The man or woman under the spell of the wolf goes out at night to a lonely spot, usually where four crossroads meet. He or she turns around very fast five times, then falls down howling and scratches the ground. On getting up, he or she is a wolf, who then runs around the countryside but is frightened off by the smallest glimmer of light. In fact, he or she howls mournfully if light is seen, and sympathetic people will turn out their lamps when they hear the howls.

This legend was strongest in the 1400s, and there were many reports of travelers at night frightening off werewolves just by waving their lanterns at them.

And there is a story from Poland of a werewolf who could only be pitied. A man was turned into a werewolf by a witch whose love he did not return. Although he looked just like a wolf, he didn't act like one. He never attacked animals or people and in fact hated raw flesh. He ate only milk, bread, and whatever other food he managed to steal from workers in the fields. For many years he wandered over the countryside, never sleeping a wink, until a great tiredness at last overcame him. He lay down to sleep, and when he woke up he was a man again. Without a stitch of clothing on, he rushed to his village, but so many years had passed that everything was changed. He didn't feel as if he belonged there anymore.

For every tale about a good werewolf, there are fifty stories about bad werewolves. The majority of these stories come from France, which seems to have had more than its share of werewolf troubles. There was hardly a province in the whole country that wasn't terrorized by man-animals at one time or another. One of the most famous of these creatures was the werewolf of Le Gévaudan.

On July 8, 1764, a young girl was found dead near the village of Saint Etienne de Lugardes. Her body was horribly clawed and partly eaten.

Within a week, five more children had been killed and mutilated in the same manner.

Everyone in the Le Gévaudan district was frightened. They did not know what kind of beast was on the prowl. It was not until September that anyone got a good look at it and lived to tell what he saw.

A hunter named Jean-Pierre Pourcher was out in the mountains near his cabin when he was amazed to come upon an awful-looking creature. It was about the size of a large donkey. When he first saw it, it was down on all fours. When it saw him, it rose up on its two hind legs and began to run at him. He took a shot at it, but he was shaking so much that he missed. Luckily for him, the creature turned and raced off up the mountain.

Over the next four or five months, the beast continued its attacks. The people were so terrorized that finally a man named Andre Portefaix decided to go to the king for help.

Portefaix went to the palace of King Louis XV at Versailles in January. Two weeks later, he returned with a troop of French cavalry. Its commander, Captain Jacques Duhamel, was under orders from the king to find and kill the creature and put an end to its reign of terror.

On February 6, the soldiers tracked the animal that everyone was by now calling a werewolf to its den in the mountains. The creature they found was described as large, hairy, and manlike. The soldiers shot at it as it escaped into the mountain forest, and the captain decided at least one of the bullets had found its mark. He declared the beast dead and took his men back to Versailles.

But the creature was not dead. It was quite alive and more savage than ever. Now it went right into villages and houses looking for victims. Between 1765 and 1767, hundreds of people were killed, and the two years became known in Le Gévaudan as the "time of death." Whole families were slaughtered, and whole villages became ghost towns as the people moved away to escape the beast.

At last, the Marquis d'Apcher decided to take the matter into his own hands. He called together all of the finest hunters in the district and every farmer and laborer who had the courage to help. In the middle of June 1767, between 500 and 600 men surrounded the area where the creature's lair was supposed to be. They beat the brush and pounded on tin pans to flush him out.

Jean Chastel was one of the hunters who had really come prepared. He had loaded his musket with silver bullets. (Many people believed that was the only way to kill a werewolf.) He was also carrying his prayer book.

The beast of Le Gévaudan.

He was reading from the prayer book on the night of June 17, 1767, as he rested in a clearing near the village of Le Sorge d'Auvert. Nearby he could hear the others banging on their pans and thrashing the brush. Suddenly, he heard a rustling sound. He grabbed his musket and stood up. From the brush across the clearing, a huge black shape emerged. The beast, standing upright, saw Chastel, and with a hideous roar, rushed at him.

Chastel's first shot caught the animal in the chest and caused it to drop to its knees. The second shot, aimed more carefully, drove a silver bullet right into its heart.

This time, the animal was really dead. But what kind of creature was it? Chastel said it had hooflike feet, pointed ears, and dark, tough hair all over its body. A local priest later interviewed many witnesses, but he couldn't identify the animal either. "I am mystified by the identity of the creature," he wrote. "There are rumors that a wolf carcass was paraded through the streets because the real beast was too terrible to display."

And there was another mystery to come: What happened to the creature's body? It was supposed to be taken to the king's palace at Versailles. But somehow, it never arrived.

CHAPTER VII
WEREWOLF STORIES FROM BRITAIN

There are not many werewolf stories from Britain, although there are quite a few stories about people turning into cats. But interestingly, the belief that the werewolf is very much like a vampire was held by the Normans of old England. A Norman chronicle tells how such awful noises came from the grave of King John (who reigned in the early 1200s) that the monks dug up his body and put it somewhere else, since they didn't think it ought to remain buried in sacred ground. After that people began to report seeing a large and vicious wolf, and so the legend began that after death King John had become a werewolf.

Elliott O'Donnell, author of a book on werewolves published in 1912, told of a werewolf haunting in Cumberland County, England. Local people began to wonder about a new house that had been built far away from town. Howling sounds seemed to come from it. And then, someone saw through the window of the house a strange-looking creature. Its body was nude and gray in color and looked pretty much like that of a man. But the head was that of a wolf—it had white, pointed teeth and eerie, light-colored eyes.

Soon after, someone found some bones in a cave nearby. These included the skull of a wolf and the skeleton of a man *without* a skull. These bones were burned, and after that no more howling sounds came from the new house, and its weird occupant was never seen again.

Wales is the setting of a fairly modern werewolf story. There in the late 1880s an Oxford University professor and his wife were at their summer cottage in Merionethshire. While wading in the lake nearby, the professor found what seemed to be the skull of a very large dog. He took it back to the cottage and put it on a shelf in the kitchen, intending to look at it more closely later.

That evening he went out, leaving his wife alone. Suddenly, she heard a scratching sound at the kitchen door. She went to the kitchen and was terrified to see a strange beast looking through the window. Huge, half-man, half-animal, it snarled at her, showing sharp, gleaming teeth. Its furry paws clutched at the windowsill like hands. But the most frightening thing to the woman was that the red eyes that glared at her were the eyes of a man.

When her husband came home with a friend, she told them what had happened. The two men decided to sit up and wait for the beast to return.

Several hours passed. Then the scratching at the kitchen window began again. Like the woman, they were horrified to see the face of a wolf with the red, raging eyes of a man. They grabbed guns and rushed to the door, just in time to see a huge animal disappear into the lake.

The next morning, the professor took the skull he had found and put it into a rowboat. Then he rowed a little way from shore and threw the skull as far out as he could into the water. The werewolf was never seen again.

CHAPTER VIII
WEREWOLF STORIES FROM SCANDINAVIA

The Scandinavian countries have a long history of werewolf lore. Norse sagas are full of wolf-man stories. One of the best known is the story of Sigmund the Volsung and his son Sinfjötli. The two were in a forest one day when they came upon a cottage where two men were in a deep sleep. Both were wearing big gold rings. They were kings' sons who were unlucky enough to have been put under a spell and turned into "skin-changers." Two wolf-shirts hung above them on hooks on the wall, for the spell called for them to be wolves for nine days and to go back to being humans on the tenth. (They were sleeping so soundly because being a wolf and doing all that killing was hard work.)

Sigmund and Sinfjötli put on the shirts and were immediately possessed by the same spell. Try as they might, they couldn't get the shirts off. They began to howl like wolves, and together they ran off into the forest. For nine days they slaughtered every animal they could find. On the tenth day they returned to the cottage, took off the shirts, and burned them. That way they were able to release themselves from the spell.

Donning a wolfskin and chanting a prayer before a fire was this man's method of turning himself into a werewolf.

The Swedes have traditionally suspected their Russian neighbors of wizardry. During the last war between the two countries, in 1908–1909, the Swedish province of Calmar was overrun by wolves, and the people were pretty sure the Russians had something to do with it. They decided that the Russians had turned Swedish prisoners of war into wolves and sent them home to destroy their countrymen.

One story that grew out of this belief was that a soldier in the Calmar regiment fighting in Russia had been captured and turned into a wolf. Homesick for his wife and children, he made his way from Finland to Calmar Province and was not far from his village when he was shot by a hunter. The hunter brought the wolf's body into the village and started to skin it. He was astonished to find a man's shirt under the wolf's skin. When they heard the news, the people of the village came to look. The soldier's wife came, too, and she recognized the shirt as one she had made for her husband before he went off to war.

Another Swedish story tells of a bridegroom and his friends who were riding through the woods when they were attacked by evil spirits and turned into wolves. Years later, the bridegroom's widow was walking in the same woods. Reaching the spot where her husband had been lost, she burst into tears and called out his name. In an instant, her lost husband appeared beside her in his human form. The sound of his name at the very spot where he had been bewitched had broken the evil spell.

Scandinavia is the source of one of the strangest werewolf beliefs. According to legend, at Christmastime men from all over the countryside change themselves into wolves and meet in a secret spot. Then, in a huge pack, they roam about at night attacking animals and people who are unlucky or foolish enough to be out. But people who live in wooded areas are not even safe in their homes. The wolves try to break down the doors, and if they succeed they destroy everyone inside. Then—and this is the strangest part—they break into taverns and beer cellars and drink all the beer or mead they can find.

CHAPTER IX
WEREWOLF STORIES FROM POLAND

In Poland, a traditional belief is that people become werewolves only at certain times of the year or for set periods of time. The most common times are Christmas and St. John's Day (in midsummer). As to the set periods of time when a human must assume wolf form, these vary from story to story.

In the following tale, the period is seven years. A man was put under a spell by a witch and forced to be a werewolf. But at the end of seven years the spell was suddenly lifted. The man rushed to his old home, only to find that his wife had married another man and had a child by him. Furious, the first husband cried out that he wished he were still a wolf so he could punish his wife. No sooner had he said this, than he turned back into a wolf. He attacked the wife and ate the child. Neighbors, hearing the commotion, rushed to the scene and killed the wolf. By morning, the wolf's body had again turned into the body of the man.

Seven years seems to have been a popular length of time for curses. In Ireland, people believed that the residents of a certain area became werewolves for seven years. And then there is the saying, familiar to us today, that if you break a mirror you are in for seven years of bad luck.

Other Polish legends have people doomed to be werewolves for much longer periods. Then, all of a sudden, the spell is lifted.

Some young people were dancing on the banks of the Vistula River when suddenly a wolf appeared. It seized and carried off the prettiest girl in the village. The young men ran after the wolf, but they were not armed, and it disappeared into the woods.

Fifty years later, a group of villagers were dancing on the very same spot when a forlorn-looking man with grayish skin appeared. One of the villagers recognized the man as his long-lost brother. Everyone sat down, and the man told the villagers that he had been turned into a wolf by a wicked witch many years before. Lonely, he had kidnapped a beautiful girl, but she had died of a broken heart in the forest about a year later. After that, he had turned into a savage werewolf and had killed and eaten many human beings over the years. Four years earlier he had turned back into a man, but he would soon turn into a wolf again. He had wanted to visit his home village once more before that happened. Just as he finished speaking, he sprang to his feet and instantly changed into a wolf. He ran off into the forest and was never seen again.

Brides and bridegrooms seemed to be especially popular targets of werewolf spells. At one wedding, the whole wedding party were turned into wolves by a soldier who was out for revenge because the bridegroom had once set his dogs on him. Some years later, three wolves were killed in a great hunt. After they were skinned, it was clear that they had been werewolves, for under the skin of one of them was a fiddle and the other two were wearing fancy dresses.

A witch came to another wedding. She rolled her belt up and put it on the threshold of the house, and then she poured a potion made from linden wood on the floor. When the newlyweds and their friends stepped over the threshold they were instantly turned into wolves. For the next three years they prowled and howled around the witch's house. At the end of three years the witch came out with a fur cloak and, turning the hairy side out, wrapped each werewolf in it. As soon as that was done, they all went back to their human forms. But the bridegroom's tail had been left uncovered by the cloak (maybe on purpose), and the poor man had to spend the rest of his life with a tail. This was supposed to have happened in 1821 or 1822.

CHAPTER X
WEREWOLF STORIES FROM OTHER EAST EUROPEAN COUNTRIES

Frankenstein, Dracula, and a wolfman all come together in the comedy film Abbott and Costello Meet Frankenstein *(1948).*

Eastern Europe, home of the vampire (Transylvania, in modern Rumania), also has a strong werewolf tradition. In fact, it is in the Slavic countries that the distinction between vampire and werewolf is fuzziest. The folk traditions of these countries hold that people who die in mortal sin rise from the grave in the form of werewolves.

In Hungary and also in Poland and Russia, people used to believe, too, that werewolves were born out of the witches' need for blood. It was said witches needed to suck the blood of humans born at the full of the moon. The gypsies of Hungary used to call these victims "water-casks," meaning that they were vessels of liquid to quench the thirst. Once a victim's blood had been sucked, that person took on many of the characteristics associated with werewolves. The face paled, the eyes became hollow and sunken, the lips swelled, and thirst became incurable. The creature made howling sounds and at night was likely to change into a fierce wolf. By morning the creature would look like a human being again but still could eat only raw meat and drink only blood.

Here is another story from Hungary, recorded in 1875. In Tórész, in the northern part of Hungary, a gypsy musician was killed by a mob of villagers who were convinced that his wife was a werewolf. The musician's name was Kropan, and he and his wife at one time were very poor. They were so poor, in fact, that they rarely had enough to eat. But suddenly all that seemed to change. This is the story the villagers told:

One day Kropan's wife served him a delicious meat dish but refused to tell him where she had gotten the meat. That night, Kropan pretended to be asleep and watched her slip quietly out of the house. At dawn, the door opened, and he was horrified to see a large gray wolf come in with a mangled lamb in its mouth. Kropan never said anything to his wife about what he saw. He guessed her secret, but he didn't care what she was if she could bring home meat. Soon, she was bringing home more meat than he could eat. He took it to a nearby town to sell it.

With the money he made selling meat, Kropan opened an inn where the menu was full of inexpensive meat dishes. By this time, the villagers had become suspicious. A wolf prowled the countryside, making off with everyone's livestock, while Kropan had enough meat to feed the whole town. A mob of people went to the inn and tied up the couple. Then a priest sprinkled drops of holy water on them both. As the drops touched Kropan's wife, she screamed in pain and vanished into thin air. The enraged peasants killed Kropan on the spot. Two leaders of the mob were later imprisoned for six years.

Finally, here is a "can't win" story from Eastern Europe. A man who had been accused of being a werewolf was brought in chains before a duke of Prussia. The duke did not believe in werewolves and decided to prove his point by ordering the man to change his shape right then and there. The man changed himself into a wolf. After the duke got over his astonishment, he ordered the man executed—for following orders.

CHAPTER XI
WEREWOLF STORIES FROM ITALY

A wealthy man from Salaparuta was seized by uncontrollable fits every time the moon was full. He would turn into a wolf and attack whatever he could find. Only one trusted servant knew his secret, and when the fits came on, this fellow would open a secret door that led from the palace to a narrow lane. The werewolf would bound through the door and prowl the city streets, terrorizing people for the rest of the night.

On one such night the werewolf set upon a young man who was either very brave or very drunk, for he refused to run away. Instead, he drew his sword and with two quick slashes made crisscross cuts on the creature's forehead. Three huge, thick drops of black blood gushed from the wound, and the wolf let out a howl of pain. Then its body went into convulsions, and before the young man's eyes the wolf vanished, and in its place lay the wealthy man, who happened also to be his friend. After that, the wealthy man was never again visited by the evil spell.

In Palermo there lived an extremely religious woman who was saying her prayers one night when she heard the howling of a wolf. Peering through her curtains, she saw in the moonlit courtyard a monstrous wolf. Whether it saw her or caught her scent, it made straight for her, bounding up onto the balcony outside her room with a single leap. The woman grabbed a letter-opener, and calling on the saints to help her, she plunged the blade into the creature's forehead just as it leaped at her. Black blood as thick as paste oozed out of the wound, and the wolf fell back off the balcony and limped away into the night.

The next day the woman was astonished to see three visitors at her door, carrying gifts of silks and jewelry and other expensive things. They had been sent by the prince of a reigning family in Palermo who wanted her to know he could never repay her for releasing him from the madness that he had long suffered.

CHAPTER XII
WEREWOLF STORIES FROM GERMANY

Many German folktales survive that have similar themes. For example, though told with all kinds of variations, there is the short tale of how a hay-mower (or a herdsman or a charcoal-burner) steals away from two companions who he thinks are asleep. He finds a lonely spot, puts a strip of wolfskin around himself, turns into a wolf, and then eats a foal (a baby horse).

But meanwhile, one of his friends has seen the whole thing. On the way home the werewolf, who has changed back into human form, complains of pains in his stomach, and the friend says he isn't surprised, since the man has eaten a whole foal. The wolf-man replies, "Had you said that to me back there, you would never have reached home again." Then he disappears, never to be seen or heard from again.

There are also several stories in which the use of a werewolf's first name causes a return to human shape. A farmer of Altona, part of present-day Hamburg, made a pact with the devil. In exchange for all the money he wanted, he would become a wolf on the last day of each month and kill a human being. For quite a while things went along fine, but one night he attacked an especially determined old woman. She shut her door on him, jamming him between the door and the door frame. He was so badly hurt that he barely managed to crawl home.

Since the man had failed to make his monthly kill, the devil visited him. The man had broken his contract, said the devil, and now the devil could take his soul. The man pleaded for another chance, and at the devil's command he ate his own small daughter.

About a year later, the man attacked his maid in a field, but she recognized him and called him by his first name three times. He changed back into his human shape and failed once more to make his kill.

For some reason, the maid did not report him. But she left immediately and went to Hamburg.

The devil again came after the farmer, and again the farmer bought his soul by eating his other child. But by now he was suspected of being a werewolf. His wife left him, and his neighbors wouldn't have anything to do with him. He decided to go to Hamburg and make a new life. But the inn where he decided to stay happened to be the very place where his former maid had taken a job. She recognized him and reported him to the authorities, and the devil soon had his soul.

A farmer's wife in Hesse served her husband meat at every meal and would not tell him where she got it. But he kept asking, and finally she agreed to let him see what she did. Her one condition was that he promise not to call her name while she was getting the meat.

Together they went to a nearby meadow where sheep were grazing. The woman put a belt around herself and instantly turned into a wolf. She snatched up one of the sheep and started to run off with it. But the shepherd and his dogs came hard on her heels and were about to overtake her.

Meanwhile, the husband was so frightened for his wife that he forgot all about his promise. "Oh, Margaret!" he cried, and at that moment the wolf disappeared and his wife stood there stark naked.

Usually, in these German stories, it is a belt (which used to be called a girdle) made of wolfskin that is used in the transformation from human to wolf shape. The effect is the same whether or not the wearer knows what he or she is putting on. In Ericksburg, according to one story, a public sale was held of items found abandoned in a room. Among the items were some werewolf girdles. The district administrator's assistant decided to try one on, and he immediately turned into a wolf and ran off. His boss rode after him, slashing at his back with a sword until he managed to cut the belt. It fell off, and the man's normal shape returned.

In another story a werewolf near Steena forgot to lock up his wolf-belt one day. His young son found it, put it on, and turned into a small werewolf. His father chased after him, caught him, and took off the belt before anything could happen. Afterward, the boy said that as soon as he put the belt on he felt so hungry he would have eaten anything he found.

In several German tales, a man or woman who is a werewolf takes great pains to protect the wife or husband. In one story that takes place in the village of Hindenburg in Altmark, the werewolf was so strong that it could carry a whole ox away in its jaws. This wolf-man killed and ate both animals and human beings, but he never touched his wife. He had taught her some magic words that would cause him to turn away whenever he came after her. These words were so powerful that the wolf would allow the wife to unbuckle his magic girdle so he would change back into human form.

Another story is about a farmer's wife. While she and her husband and others are gathering hay in the fields one day, she tells her husband that she is so restless she cannot stay in the fields any longer. Before she leaves, she makes him promise that if any wild beast tries to attack him he will throw his hat at it and run away. Not long after the woman leaves, a wolf comes swimming across the nearby river and attacks the man. He throws his hat at the wolf, and the animal tears it to shreds. But another man sneaks up on the wolf from behind and stabs it with his pitchfork. As the wolf falls, it disappears, and lying on the ground dead is the farmer's wife.

In still another story of this kind, a farmer and his wife are driving through the woods, when the farmer suddenly stops and gets down from the wagon. He tells his wife to drive on and that if any beast attacks her she is to throw her apron at it. Pretty soon a wolf comes out of the woods and heads for the woman in the wagon. She throws her apron at it and races off, leaving the wolf busily tearing the apron to pieces. When her husband returns she guesses his secret, for between his teeth are threads from her apron.

It is not told what happened to the couple after that. In werewolf stories, spouses seem to react in a variety of ways. Some just accept the fact that they are married to werewolves, others try to do away with them, and at least one horrified wife is said to have up and died on the spot.

CHAPTER XIII
WEREWOLF STORIES FROM FRANCE

France is especially rich in werewolf lore. Here is just a sampling of the many stories:

In Auvergne in the early 1220s, a certain nobleman banished a soldier named Rimbaud de Poiret. The poor man did not want to leave his home and could not bring himself to make a new home anywhere else. So he wandered all alone for months. His clothes became torn and dirty and his hair and beard grew long, and after a time he became frightening to look at. Then one night, to his amazement, he turned into a wolf.

The first thing he did as a wolf was to go back to his native village and attack every man, woman, and child he could find. Children were eaten up in a few gulps, and even adults were partly eaten by this beast-marauder. The town was terrorized.

At last a brave carpenter took a stand against the monster, and with his axe cut off one of the wolf's hind paws. Instantly, the wolf turned into Rimbaud, who thanked the carpenter over and over for releasing him from his cursed wolf form.

A great lord of Brittany had everything, including a wife who adored him. One thing troubled the wife, though. For three days each week he disappeared and would not say where he went. She begged and pleaded with him to tell her and finally he did.

He was a werewolf for those three days, he said, and he lived in the forest and hunted for raw flesh. To turn into a werewolf he had to be naked. So he always went to an old hut and took off his clothes and hid them under a stone. It was very important that the clothes remain untouched, he told her, because if they were taken away he would be doomed forever to remain a wolf.

The wife was disgusted by what she heard. She could not love a werewolf. After a time she talked a knight who was in love with her into going to the secret place and stealing the clothes. Sure enough, her husband did not come back after the three days. The wife married the knight, and they enjoyed her former husband's land and wealth. But eventually the plot was discovered. The knight had not thought to destroy the lord's clothes, and, at last, wolf and clothes were reunited and the lord returned to human form.

Around 1530, the people of Poitiers began to talk about the goings-on at an old chateau nearby. Three young men decided to see for themselves, and so one Friday at midnight they stole up to the chateau and peered through a crack in one of the window shutters. There inside were several witches conducting some sorcery. Frightened, the youths turned to run away, but they were set upon by three fierce wolves. They drew their swords and fought the wolves back, and one youth managed to slice off the ear of one of the animals. The next day the swordsman learned that a woman of the town, who was suspected of witchcraft, had lost an ear.

The belief has long been held in many parts of France, but especially in Brittany, that wizards exist who lead werewolf packs on their nighttime raids. Sometimes the wizard himself turns into a wolf, but he always speaks with a human voice, even in his wolf form. He tells the other werewolves what farms are poorly guarded at night, what flocks and herds are not looked after properly, and which paths are most likely to be taken by nighttime wayfarers. Then he plunges into the woods with the wolf-pack behind him, to begin a night of marauding.

One night in the mid-1800s, two men were crossing a forest when they stopped short at the edge of a clearing. There in the moonlight stood an old man they knew, and he was making strange signs in the air with his hands. The two men hid themselves behind a tree, and soon they saw thirteen wolves emerge from the forest into the clearing. The leader of the pack, a large gray wolf, went right up to the man and allowed the man to pet him. Then the man began a sing-song chant, and moments later he plunged into the forest, followed by the wolves.

CHAPTER XIV
PERSECUTION OF WEREWOLVES

Most of the werewolf legends that survive today come from Europe in the 1500s and 1600s. At no other time in history were people so terrified of werewolves or so convinced that werewolves were just about everywhere, lying in wait to kill and maim innocent victims.

And, at no other time in history were people who were suspected of being werewolves persecuted so harshly. It was during this same period that people believed so strongly in witches and held the greatest number of witch trials.

Some students of history say that the Roman Catholic Church brought this about. It was in the 1500s that Protestantism was born and that many people began to grow disillusioned with the Catholic Church. Desperate to keep the people loyal, the Church started saying that devils and demons were at work among them.

Other scholars say that the people of Europe led such hard and tragic lives that only the existence of devils and demons in their midst could explain the misery. These historians say that there is a clear relationship between tragic lives and a belief in witchcraft. For example, any culture where many babies die is likely to have a strong belief in monsters and spirits that kill babies. This is true of primitive cultures even today. When modern medicine is brought to these people and the rate of infant death begins to drop, the belief in witchcraft becomes less strong.

Whatever the reasons, if you lived in Europe in the 1500s and 1600s, you would probably have believed in werewolves and witches. You would have been very suspicious of anyone in town who had a lot of hair or pointed teeth or who acted strangely when the moon was full. And you would have been in real danger if you looked or acted like that. You might very well have wound up as a defendant in an inquisition.

Inquisitions were investigations by the Roman Catholic Church. They were like trials, and they were held to decide if a particular behavior or belief went against the teachings of the Church.

There were inquisitions way back in the 400s, but these were usually local affairs. It was in 1199 that Pope Innocent III began to send inquisitors, or judges, directly from the Vatican in Rome. The Inquisition, with a capital *I*, dates from that time.

This is the way the inquisitions worked:

1. Those accused were presumed to be guilty until they could prove their innocence. (In our legal system, it's just the opposite.)
2. Gossip and suspicion were enough to cause someone to be formally accused.
3. Witnesses and accusers did not have to identify themselves. Often, even their charges were not made known to the defendant.
4. No witnesses were allowed to testify for the accused.
5. The accused could not have a lawyer.
6. Although torture was supposed to be used only as a last resort, actually it was used all the time—on both witnesses and defendants.
7. Once defendants had confessed (and they usually did

under torture), they had to give the names of others who had helped them.
8. As a rule, defendants could not change their minds or take back their confessions.
9. Anyone convicted was almost automatically sentenced to death.

Needless to say, not many people survived an inquisition.

It would be unfair not to mention that other churches have been just as harsh at certain times in their history. In the late 1500s, while the Catholic states in Germany were persecuting witches, the Protestant states were doing the same thing. In Protestant Saxony, in the town of Quedlinburg, 133 witches were burned in a single day in 1589. Since the town's population was only 12,000, that's almost ten percent of all the people who lived there. The witch trials in Salem, Massachusetts, in the 1600s, were conducted not by Catholics but by Puritans.

Trials of witches became a part of the Inquisition in Europe in the 1200s. The first woman was burned for witchcraft in France in 1275. In 1320, Pope John XXIV decreed that anyone who worshipped demons, entered into a pact with them, made images, or used sacred objects to work magic should be tried as heretics, or enemies of the Church.

Although suspected witches were tried here and there over the next one hundred and fifty-odd years, it was not until the late 1400s that the Inquisition began to try large numbers of people for witchcraft and sorcery. And it was not until the early 1500s that the Inquisition began to use these trials as a major political weapon.

People were revolting against the Church. The Church fought back by saying that witches and sorcerers were to blame. But a man who has studied witchcraft has another idea. Rossell Robbins says that the inquisitors did such a good job of stamping out other kinds of heresy by around 1300 that they suddenly found themselves with nothing more to do. "Witchcraft was in fact *invented* to fill the gap."

Since werewolves were thought to be in the same class as witches, it was not long before inquisitors in some parts of Europe started holding a lot of werewolf trials.

In Eastern Europe between 1520 and the mid-1600s there were 30,000 werewolf trials. It is not known just how many were held in Western Europe in the same years, but there were a lot, especially in France and Germany.

In the following chapters, we will look at some of the more famous werewolf cases.

CHAPTER XV
THE CASE OF PETER STUMP

Probably the most famous werewolf case comes from Germany. Not only was it the most famous case, but also the man who was accused was punished more harshly than any other suspected werewolf in history.

The man's name was Peter Stump (or Stubb), and he was arrested and brought to trial in Cologne in 1590. He told the judges that he had made a pact with the devil and that the devil had given him a wolfskin belt. Whenever he put it on, he turned into a wolf. Whenever he took it off, he became a man again.

His first victim was his infant son. But there would be many more victims in the years that followed. According to an English pamphlet published about him in the year of his trial:

> He would walk up and down, and if he could spy either maid, wife, or child that his eyes liked and his heart lusted after, he would wait their issuing out of the city or town, if he could by any means get them alone, he would in the fields ravish them.

Within a few years, according to the pamphlet, he had murdered thirteen children and two women. He also claimed to have killed and eaten some cattle and sheep, and to have killed men who were his enemies, although he did not eat them. By the time he was arrested and brought to trial, he had been a werewolf for twenty-five years.

There were many attempts to hunt down the terrible wolf that was thought to be responsible for so many killings. Finally, a group of men and dogs lay in wait one night, and when they saw the wolf they went after him. What they found was Peter Stump, and they decided that was too much of a coincidence. They took him to the authorities.

The main evidence against Peter Stump was circumstantial. No one had actually seen him in the shape of a wolf, but he was found in the very place where a wolf had just been. There was also his confession. But the judges at the trial found it hard to check on the facts it contained. For instance, Stump said he had left his magic belt in a certain valley. But though they searched the whole valley, they could not find it. They decided that the devil must have taken it back, since Peter Stump had no more use for it.

For his crimes, Peter Stump was tortured to death and then his body was burned to ashes.

CHAPTER XVI
THREE WEREWOLF CASES IN FRANCE

By far the greatest number of werewolf trials in Western Europe took place in France. Here are just three of many.

In the Poligny district of the country, in 1521, a traveler passing through was attacked by a wolf. He managed to wound the animal, and he followed its trail to a nearby hut. There, he found Michel Verdun hurt, his wounds being tended by his wife.

The traveler reported what had happened to the police, and Verdun was arrested. Under torture he said that he had kept another man faithful to the devil. This man, Pierre Bourgot, was also arrested and tortured until he confessed.

Pierre Bourgot told how, back in 1502, a bad storm had scattered his sheep. While searching for them, he had met three dark horsemen. He told them his troubles, and one of them promised to help Bourgot if he would serve the horseman as his lord and master. Soon, Bourgot found his sheep. He later found out that the horseman was a servant of the devil. Bourgot denied Christianity and became a servant of the devil, too.

After two years, Bourgot began to drift back to Christianity. Sensing this, the devil's servants told Michel Verdun to make sure Pierre remained loyal.

Verdun took Bourgot to a witches' meeting where, according to Bourgot, everyone carried a green candle burning with a blue flame. Then Verdun told Bourgot to take off all his clothes and to smear a magic ointment over his body. To his astonishment, Bourgot found that he had turned into a wolf. Two hours later Verdun gave him another ointment to put on his body, to change it back into human form. From then on, Pierre confessed, he changed into a wolf often.

He had once attacked a seven-year-old boy. But the victim had screamed so loudly that Bourgot got frightened and put his clothes back on so that no one would detect him. But he had been successful with other children, including a four-year-old girl and a nine-year-old girl.

Both Michel Verdun and Pierre Bourgot were found guilty and were burned.

At Dole in 1573, a man named Gilles Garnier was accused of being a werewolf. Several witnesses swore that he had eaten an eleven-year-old girl in a nearby wood. Other witnesses said that eight days before All Saints Day (our Halloween), he attacked another young girl. She was rescued by some passersby, but she died a few days later from her injuries.

A couple of weeks after that, he was supposed to have strangled and eaten part of the body of a ten-year-old boy.

What is remarkable about this case is that Garnier was accused of doing this sort of thing even in human form. Neighbors said he had strangled a boy in the woods and would have eaten him if they hadn't stopped him.

After fifty witnesses had testified against him, Gilles Garnier was tortured into confessing. He was put on a rack, and his body was pulled from both ends until he couldn't stand the pain any longer and admitted his guilt. Then, as was the custom, he was made to repeat his confession so that it could be recorded as having been given freely.

Then the court gave its verdict:

> Seeing that Gilles Garnier has, by the testimony of credible witnesses, and by his own spontaneous confession, been proven guilty of the abominable crimes of lycanthropy and witchcraft, the court condemns him, the said Gilles, to be this day taken in a cart from this spot to the place of execution... where he... shall be tied to a stake and burned alive, and that his ashes be then scattered to the winds. The court further condemns him, the said Gilles, to the costs of this prosecution.

In other words, not only was he going to have to die horribly, but also he was going to have to pay all the costs of his own trial, torture, and execution.

In 1598 in St. Claude in the Jura region of France, a whole family was accused of being werewolves—two sisters, a brother, and his son. The first sister, Perrenette Gandillon, was killed by a mob of angry peasants who found her in the area where a murder had just been committed. The other three members of the family were arrested and tried together.

Antoinette, the second sister, was accused not just of being a werewolf but also of making hail, attending witches' meetings, and sleeping with the devil.

Her brother Pierre, accused also of werewolfism and witchcraft, confessed that the devil clothed his family in wolfskins that completely covered them and that they ran around the countryside on all fours, killing animals or humans, depending on what they had a taste for at the time. Then Pierre's son, George, also confessed to covering himself with ointment and turning into a wolf.

The judge visited the three people in jail. He reported, "I have seen [them] go on all fours in a room just as they did when they were in the fields; but they said that it was impossible for them to turn themselves into wolves, since they had no more ointment, and they had lost the power of doing so by being imprisoned."

All three were convicted and burned. Before the series of trials connected with this family came to an end, a total of eight people had been executed.

CHAPTER XVII
HOW TO BECOME A WEREWOLF

In most of the werewolf films, the werewolves do not want to change from people to beasts. They stare with disbelief at their hands as their nails grow longer and fur sprouts from their knuckles. They run to a mirror and are horrified to see their human features turning into those of a wolf. But in a few minutes the feeling of horror has ended, for their human brain has become a beast's brain, and all they can think about is their desire for flesh. After a night of killing and rampaging, they wake up human again and are not even sure if what happened to them the night before was real or just an awful dream.

This is not what most people believed happened in the days when the belief in werewolves was widespread. Instead, they believed that the majority of werewolves wanted to be able to change from human to beast and would go through all kinds of rituals to do so. In fact, they believed that you had to go through these rituals unless some special condition caused you to be a werewolf against your will.

The modern idea that most werewolves get that way without trying did exist in Europe hundreds of years ago. You could be the son or daughter of a werewolf and so inherit

*Lon Chaney, Jr.,
in another scene from
The Wolfman.*

the condition. Or, you could be conceived at the time of the full moon. You could even become a werewolf if you were careless or stupid enough to sleep overnight in the open on a Friday under a full moon.

In France especially some people believed that a priest's curse could turn a person into a werewolf for three or seven years. Also in France, at the beginning of the nineteenth century, it was believed that at each full moon some young men, especially the sons of priests, were turned into werewolves.

In both Italy and Scandinavia, people believed that if you were born on Christmas night you were doomed to turn into a wolf for eight days at Christmastime each year.

In Sicilian tradition, a child conceived at the time of a new moon would become a werewolf, and so would a man who slept out in the open, with the moon shining full on his face, on a certain Wednesday or Friday in summer. (This may be related to the belief that werewolves change shape on St. John's Day in midsummer.)

In some areas, the belief existed that one person could make another person believe he or she had changed into an animal or bird. There were prescriptions for doing this. One calls for putting mandrake, stramonium or solanum manicum, belladonna, and henbane into a cup of wine. It was said that after drinking such a mixture a person would think he or she was everything from a fish to a goose.

Another prescription says to "seethe in a brazen vessel" the fat of young children, skim off the scum, and add hemlock, aconite, poplar leaves, and soot. And still another calls for a mixture of cowbane, sweet flag, cinquefoil, bat's blood, deadly nightshade, and oil.

Some of these ingredients are really powerful drugs, especially if you drink them. If rubbed on the skin, they are better absorbed when mixed with fat of some kind. Witches and sorcerers apparently knew that, since many of the recipes for ointments call for an ingredient like "the fat of young children." It's likely that they didn't really use this ingredient very often and just said the fat or oil they were using came from that source. Notice the prescription that just calls for "oil."

Belladonna, or deadly nightshade, is a powerful poison that acts on the nervous system. A large dose can cause a person to become very talkative, laugh a lot, get very excited, and see visions. Henbane in large doses produces hallucinations.

Hemlock in large doses leads to a loss of muscle power and, eventually, paralysis.

Aconite, a root also called monk's hood, also acts on the nervous system and causes tingling sensations and numbness.

No doubt about it, these early witches knew a great deal about the properties of various plants.

The greatest number of prescriptions and rituals for turning a person into a werewolf show that people believed werewolves generally wanted to be the way they were and would do some pretty odd things to become that way.

Often, shape-changing was seen as just another activity of witches, and werewolfery and witchery are linked together in much of European folklore. Many stories about witches' get-togethers tell how the witches all rode to the meeting places on the backs of wolves. Sometimes all the witches would then turn into wolves and roam the countryside, killing herds of sheep and cattle. In addition, the way to become a werewolf was frequently the same as the way to become a witch—by making a pact with the devil.

But there are many stories and reports of werewolves that were only werewolves. They could not fly or do sorcery and magic like witches could. Their only power was the ability to change themselves from humans to beasts. That called for different rituals than entering into a contract with the devil.

The most complicated prescription was this: On the night of a full moon, go to a lonely hilltop. There, at midnight, draw two circles on the ground, one inside the other. The outer circle must measure 7 feet (2.1 m) across, the inner circle 3 feet (0.9 m) across. Inside the smaller circle build a fire, and set an iron pot on an iron stand over the fire. Boil water in the pot and put herbs into it to make a potion. Any three of the following herbs can be used: hemlock, opium, henbane, parsley, saffron, aloe, poppyseed, solanum, asafetida. As the ingredients blend together, speak some magic words. Just what the words are varies depending on the source, but they are from a poem that goes something like this:

> *Spirits of the deep*
> *Who never sleep,*
> *Be kind to me.*
>
> *Spirits from the grave*
> *Without a soul to save,*
> *Be kind to me.*
>
> *Spirits of the trees*
> *That grow upon the lees,*
> *Be kind to me.*
>
> *Spirits of the dead*
> *That glide with noiseless tread,*
> *Be kind to me.*
>
> *Wolves, vampires, satyrs, ghosts!*
> *Elect of all the devilish hosts!*
>
> *I pray you send hither,*
> *Send hither, send hither,*
> *The great gray shape that makes men shiver!*

Then, take off all your clothes and smear your whole body with a special ointment. Few of the stories tell exactly what is in the ointment, but it is a blend of poisons and other deadly substances and is either black or a sickening shade of green. One account describes the potion as made up of animal fat and camphor, anise and opium.

After that, put on either a wolfskin belt or the hide of a wolf. Kneel down inside the large circle but outside the small circle (you may be snatched away by the spirits inside the small one) and wait. If you have done everything correctly, a demon will appear in the inner circle and grant you the power to change into a wolf whenever you want to.

In Norway and Sweden, where the female werewolf was believed to be as common as the male, there was a special prescription to be used by a woman who wanted to become a werewolf. She had to go to a magic river at midnight when the moon was full and speak some magic words to call forth the spirits who could give her the werewolf power.

Then she had to touch the riverbank three times with her forehead and dunk her head in the water three times. Each time she put her head in the water she was supposed to take a mouthful of it. She repeated this dunking and swallowing process until the demon came to her. It could take up to twenty-four hours.

In Russia you had to go to the stump of an aspen tree at the full of the moon and speak a chant that included these lines: "Moon, moon! Golden horns! Melt the bullet, blunt the knife, rot the cudgel, strike fear into man, beast, and reptile, so that they may not seize the gray wolf, nor tear from him his warm hide."

In some areas you didn't have to go through nearly as much rigamarole. In fact, turning yourself into a werewolf was so easy that it's a wonder all the would-be werewolves didn't just go to those areas for their transformation.

By some accounts, all you had to do was go to a lonely spot at the full of the moon, take off all your clothes, and roll around in the dirt for a few minutes.

It was very important that no one tamper with your clothes while you were out being a wolf, though. In Ireland, when werewolves wanted to transform themselves, it was believed that they left their whole human bodies behind and warned their friends not to move or touch the bodies or else they would not be able to return to human form.

In the Balkan region of southern Europe, you could become a werewolf by eating a certain flower that was variously identified as a yellow snapdragon, a large red daisy, or a dead white sunflower with a sickly smell.

Many people throughout Europe believed you could become a werewolf by drinking water from a wolf's pawprint. And the belief that you could turn into a werewolf by eating the meat of a sheep that had been killed by a wolf was so widespread that in some areas laws were passed against eating the flesh of any animal killed by a wolf.

In Scandinavia, it was believed that people skilled in witchcraft merely had to say the words of a spell while drinking a cup of ale.

In parts of France, it was believed that if you stopped taking Communion or using holy water for ten years, you would become a werewolf.

In Russia, you could become a werewolf by going into a forest, finding a tree that had been cut down, and plunging a small copper knife into it.

In Iceland, all you had to do was put a wolf's skin over your body.

In Germany in ancient times, a wolfskin shirt was enough, and later on just a belt would do. The belt didn't even have to be made out of a wolf's skin, for the skin of a man who had been hanged would do just as well. But the belt had to be fastened with a buckle having seven tongues.

In other areas, the belt had to be "three fingers wide," and if it were made from human skin it had to be from a criminal who had been tortured to death.

Apparently, Peter Stump, or Stubb, the famous werewolf in Germany, took the hard route. He made a pact with the devil, who then gave him a wolfskin belt. But it seems that would-be werewolves in other parts of Germany didn't have to bother with devil pacts.

With so many ways to become a werewolf, no wonder there were so many of them around.

CHAPTER XVIII
HOW TO SPOT A WEREWOLF

Even today, we are likely to look at certain people and say (or at least think) that they look like werewolves. Someone must have said that to the radio and television personality who calls himself "Wolfman Jack." He was probably a pretty ordinary-looking man until he grew a beard. When someone said, "You look like a werewolf," he may have decided it would be a good gimmick, a way to make himself known and to get ahead in show business. He started calling himself "Wolfman Jack," and the gimmick has worked very well for him.

This author remembers a college student who worked with children one summer. He had thick dark eyebrows and a heavy black beard. One of the kids started calling him "Wolfman," and pretty soon the other children were doing the same. He tried to laugh it off, but he didn't really like being called "Wolfman."

Nowadays, if you happen to have certain physical characteristics, the worst that can happen to you is that someone will make you feel uncomfortable by saying you look like a werewolf. But back in the days when people believed in werewolves, you could be in real trouble.

A terrifying moment from the film,
I Was a Teenage Werewolf (1957).

Other people would be very suspicious of you. And one day you might find yourself being arrested and brought to trial.

Several hundred years ago, if you happened to have dark eyebrows that met at the bridge of your nose, you were automatically a suspicious character. If you also had a beard, that was even more proof of your probable werewolfhood. But there were many other signs:

- *Long, pointed teeth.* If they were black or reddish, you were even more suspect. But they could also be gleaming white.
- *Pawlike hands.* They should be broad in the palm, and very hairy. If the fingers were short and the fingernails long and curving, so much the worse. One convicted werewolf, who was sentenced to prison, was said to have had nails that were black and worn away in places, as if from clawing at things. An especially long third finger was also suspect.
- *Small ears set low on the head.* Wolves have short ears, so naturally werewolves would, too.
- *Pale eyes, especially greenish-yellow ones.* Eyes that glowed red in firelight. Also, eyes that were hot and dry (werewolves are not supposed to be able to cry).
- *Extreme hairiness.* People with a lot of body hair were thought to be closer to the animal world than people without much hair.
- *Pale skin.* This was a suspicious trait because werewolves were supposed to prefer the night and not like sunlight.
- *Deepset eyes.*
- *A hatred for bright light.* This was a sure sign of werewolfhood.
- *A tendency toward dryness in the mouth.* There is a connection here with real wolves. Many real wolves were rabid; one of the symptoms of rabies is mouth dryness.
- *A fear of water.* Another symptom of rabies is a dread of water. In fact, the medical term for rabies is *hydrophobia*, an extreme fear of water.
- *A liking for rare or raw meat.* Most people still like their meat well done. Even today, anyone who likes steak tartare

(a raw ground-meat dish) is an object of suspicion to many people.
- *A habit of showing up with thorn scratches or dog bites—* sure signs that you've been doing something suspicious.
- *A wound in the same part of the body where a wolf was recently wounded.* As we have learned, people believed that any injury done to a werewolf in wolf form would remain after the werewolf changed back into human form.
- *Just being in the wrong place at the wrong time.* If you happened to be in an area where a wolf had just attacked someone or some animal, you were liable to be blamed for the wolf's attack.

If you have any of these physical traits or have ever been in a situation like the last three described above, just think how lucky you are to be living now instead of a few hundred years ago. Even one of these characteristics or situations was enough to put a person in danger if he or she happened to live in an area where wolves were on the attack, where children were being killed in great numbers, or where sheep and cattle were being found dead. As we have seen, anything like this was accepted as damaging evidence during the time of the werewolf trials.

CHAPTER XIX
PROTECTION AGAINST WEREWOLVES

Any culture that is rich in the folklore of the supernatural will also be rich in remedies for protection against the supernatural. And so in Europe hundreds of years ago there were all kinds of ways to protect yourself against werewolves and other demons.

Certain herbs were thought to be powerful. Vampires hated garlic, it was believed, so smart people hung garlic in their homes to keep vampires away. There were also several plants that were said to give protection against werewolves.

In Britain these included rye, mistletoe, ash, and yew. You could plant rye in your yard and put in ash and yew trees. You could hang mistletoe in your house. Nowadays, we still hang mistletoe in our houses at Christmastime, but we do it to encourage people to kiss each other. A few hundred years ago, people did the same thing to keep werewolves away.

In Scandinavia it was believed that werewolves were especially active around Christmastime. The same belief was held in parts of Britain. There, it was the custom to burn an ash log at Christmastime. Among other things, the British believed that no meat-eating animal would come around an ash tree or a burning ash log.

In Italy there were a couple of things you could do if a werewolf came knocking at your door. You could wait until he or she knocked three times. Three was a good-magic number, and you could let a werewolf in after the third knock without worrying that he or she would hurt you. If you were too frightened to wait for the third knock, you could drive the werewolf away by throwing a key of a certain shape at him or her.

Some people believed that if you saw a werewolf, all you had to do to protect yourself was stick your sword into the ground, with the handle embedded in the earth and the point aimed toward the wolf. This "banned" the wolf, which could not come back again except as a person.

In most places where people believed in werewolves they also believed that the creatures were afraid of running water. As mentioned earlier, this belief probably had to do with the fact that many real wolves had rabies, and so people assumed werewolves did, too. (Rabies = hydrophobia = fear of water.) At some point in history, people noticed that rabid wolves ran away from running water and decided that werewolves must have the same fear. Many people built their houses on rivers or streams because of this belief.

The religious meaning of running water probably also has something to do with this belief. There is something about running water that has always made people think of life and renewal. Water was important in ancient religions long before Christianity. Then, when Christianity came along, water was an important part of the first sacrament—baptism.

Running water was used as a test in cases of witchcraft and sorcery as far back as 3,000 B.C. in Babylon. It was important in ancient England for proving guilt or innocence, not just in cases of witchcraft but for stealing and killing and other crimes. The belief in the water test was so strong that it was even used in the Salem, Massachusetts, witch trials in the 1690s.

The water test is very simple. You put the suspect into a stream or lake or tub of water. If the suspect sank, he or she was innocent. If the suspect floated, he or she was guilty.

The trouble was, the witnesses to the test usually waited quite a while to make sure of what they saw. People who sank into the water could drown before they were brought up.

This practice was called "swimming a witch" in England and Germany in the seventeenth century. It is not hard to understand why people in these countries stopped swimming during this time. Someone might see them paddling around and decide that, since they didn't sink, they were witches.

Finally, the very symbol of Christianity, the cross, could be used against werewolves, just as it could be used against other demons, such as vampires.

Remember that in all the vampire films people arm themselves with crosses. The Europeans did the same thing when they came up against werewolves. In most parts of Europe the cross could be wooden or metal. In some parts of Italy it had to be made of wax, and it had to be blessed by a priest on Ascension Day. These crosses were then placed on doors and roadside shrines. If a werewolf came near one of these crosses, it was believed that all power would leave him or her, and he or she would slink away.

Of course, more regular means of protection were used, too. Werewolves were not immune to guns, knives, or clubs. Many stories tell how people were able to injure werewolves with such weapons. If you were brave enough and strong enough, your ordinary weapons were probably the best protection against werewolves. Not only did they cause the werewolf to run away, but if you managed to wound the werewolf you had a good chance of finding out who he or she was in human form.

People just about everywhere believed that the wound would still be there even if the werewolf changed back. There is a sixteenth-century French legend about a hunter who was attacked by a wolf and who fought back, cutting off one of the animal's paws. He put the paw in his hunting sack and set off for home.

On the way he met a friend and told him what had just happened. Reaching into his sack to show the paw as proof, he pulled out not a wolf's paw but a woman's hand. On one of the fingers was a familiar gold ring. When he arrived home he found his wife bandaging the stump of her arm. He reported her to the authorities and she was tried and executed as a werewolf.

So, if you could wound a werewolf, you could probably identify him or her later. You couldn't do that with crosses or burning ash logs or keys. The best protection against werewolves, in most people's opinion, was finding them out and killing them.

CHAPTER XX
HOW TO KILL A WEREWOLF

Considering how savage and powerful werewolves were supposed to be, it seems odd that the people of Europe had so little trouble killing them. In many werewolf legends, the creatures were killed in the same way ordinary wolves were. Men went after them with dogs and guns and clubs, cornered them, and killed them.

Usually in these tales, once the werewolf was wounded or dead, it automatically changed back into human form. There are no legends about a werewolf caught in human form escaping by turning into a wolf. That is one of the more puzzling things about the werewolf trials in Europe.

Imagine a crowded courtroom. The judges are sitting on their high bench. One by one, witnesses are called to testify against the accused. Suddenly, the prisoner begins to shake all over. He falls to the floor, writhing in pain. Then, before everyone's eyes, he turns into a wolf. Snarling and snapping, he frightens everyone back, then runs howling from the room.

But this never happened. The people who were convicted as werewolves and executed by fire seem to have died like perfectly ordinary human beings. Their supernatural powers appear to have deserted them completely. It was the same with convicted witches.

People did wonder about that. But since they certainly did not want to believe they had had any part in the death of innocent men and women they came up with an explanation. The devil, they said, deserted werewolves who were caught. His whole point in turning them into werewolves in the first place was to get their souls. When a werewolf was captured, it just meant that its soul would be coming to him earlier than expected.

The most common method of killing a werewolf, then, was public execution carried out by civil or religious authorities.

Of course the populace could not always rely on the authorities to catch and execute werewolves. Sometimes other means of killing them had to be employed. In addition to ordinary means, there were some magical methods.

Remember the vampire films where the vampire can only be killed by a wooden stake driven through his heart? That was a Russian belief. In fact, in Russian folklore, both buried vampires *and* buried werewolves had to be killed in that way.

Most cultures did not believe werewolves remained alive after burial or that they returned from the dead. But clearly people in Russia did. The stake had to be made of aspen wood. It is interesting to remember that the Russian prescription for turning into a werewolf that we gave earlier specified going to the stump of an aspen tree at the full moon.

There was one method of killing a werewolf that was actually more like a cure, for it killed only the werewolf and not the person. You had to shoot the werewolf with a silver bullet.

So the Lone Ranger was not the first hero to use silver bullets. In fact, the inventor of the Lone Ranger character must have read the werewolf myths of England and Scotland. In Russia and elsewhere, people believed that a silver bullet, especially one blessed by a priest, could be a wonderful weapon of mercy. Just shoot the werewolf with it and you save a perfectly nice human being from a tragic double life.

Of course the devil did not like the idea that a single well-aimed silver bullet could undo all his work. In at least one prescription for becoming a werewolf, there is a magical incantation against this weapon. It is that same prescription from Russian folklore that specified doing the ritual by an aspen tree. Part of that chant went: "Melt the bullet, blunt the knife..."

But the devil did not have to worry all that much about the power of the bullet. Most people did not go around with silver bullets in their guns. And the authorities don't appear to have taken the trouble to deal with werewolves in this sympathetic way. It was usually only a brave loved one who went to this kind of trouble to kill the werewolf and save the person trapped inside its body.

CHAPTER XXI
HOW TO CURE A WEREWOLF

Even in those places where no one believed in the power of silver bullets (or didn't have any), people did believe that there were ways to cure werewolves without killing them.

The most common belief was that all you had to do was to *undo* whatever had made the werewolf become a werewolf in the first place.

In most of the modern horror films, the werewolf doesn't do much of anything. He or she changes into a wolf without expecting it, and when the night is over, changes back. The idea that werewolves automatically changed back to human shape at sunrise was fairly widespread in Europe hundreds of years ago. But there were also many people who believed the werewolf had to go through some kind of ritual to change back into a human being.

If you had smeared a special ointment on your body to change yourself into a wolf, you had to smear a different salve on yourself to change back into a person. If you'd rolled in the dirt to become a wolf, you had to bathe in running water to become human again. (Obviously, the people who

Most people were able to become werewolves without much trouble. However, in the film The Werewolf of London *(1935), Henry Hull, who played the demon, had to concoct a potion in his laboratory to turn himself into an animal.*

believed this didn't believe that werewolves were afraid of running water.) If you'd put on a wolfskin belt to become a werewolf, you had to remove the belt to change back into a person.

What is a little hard to understand is that if the werewolf could do that kind of thing alone, why would he or she be cured if someone else did it? The explanation is probably that it depended on *attitude*. The other person would bring good intention to the magic. Anyway, the other person did not owe anything to the devil and so could work against him better.

Other cures range from the very simple to the very complex. Here are some simple ones:

- Prick the werewolf in its wolf form and make it bleed.
- Pierce the back of its front paws, and the spell will be broken.
- Hit the werewolf on the forehead or scalp three times, each time drawing one drop of blood.
- Throw pieces of clothing at it. These will remind the werewolf of its human form.
- Call the werewolf by its human name three times. The name itself has the power to cure. This was a common belief in Germany.

According to some legends, you did not even have to use the name, just recognize who the wolf really was. One such legend tells of a farmer who was plowing with his horse in a field when a wolf appeared and began to attack the horse. The farmer thought there was something familiar about the wolf's growls and howls, and at last he cried, "Is that you, my old mother?" Instantly the wolf vanished, and there stood his mother.

In some areas of Denmark people believed that all you had to do was shout at a wolf that you suspected was a werewolf: "You are not a wolf. You are a werewolf!" If the wolf was indeed a werewolf, it would be cured, and you would be safe. If it was a real wolf, you would probably be in trouble.

In parts of Italy, it was believed that if you could draw a cross, or an X, on the forehead of the werewolf you could free him or her from the spell. There is a story in Italian folklore, very similar to some of the ones mentioned earlier, about a young man who fought back when a wolf attacked him. He took out his sword and slashed an X on the creature's brow, and huge black glops of blood came out of the wound. The werewolf went into a fit of agony and then vanished, leaving in its place a good friend of the young swordsman. Without even knowing it, the swordsman had freed his friend from the curse of werewolfhood.

A similar cure calls for throwing iron or steel at the wolf. The skin on its forehead then splits crosswise, and the naked person comes out through the opening.

In those areas where people believed a person turned into a werewolf because of a priest's curse, it was also believed that the werewolf could be cured if wounded in wolf form by that or any other priest.

There are also cases here and there about werewolves being cured through exorcism. A case in France reported in the early 1200s has to do with a priest who cured a werewolf in this way. He heard about a werewolf in a nearby village, journeyed there, and found the people alarmed and fearful. He told them that the man needed help, and he then led them straight to the forest spot where the poor man lay in a trance. The priest woke him up and ordered him to change into a wolf, which the man did. The priest then exorcised the werewolf, explaining to the astounded people that although a man's body could be changed into that of a wolf, a man's soul could never enter such a body.

In Greece, if a man could be kept from eating meat for nine years, he would be cured at the end of that time; and in Ireland the same was true for seven years.

One of the strangest cures of all comes from German folklore. To work it, you had to know who the werewolf was in human form. Once you'd found that out, all you had to do was shift its belt buckle to the ninth hole.

Here are a few of the more complicated cures:

Catch a werewolf in its wolf form. Find three (brave) girls and give them twigs from an ash tree. Tell them to hit the wolf with the twigs and chant:

> *Gray wolf ugly, gray wolf old,*
> *Do at once as you are told.*
> *Leave this man and fly away—*
> *Right away, far away,*
> *Where it's night and never day.*

If you can't find three girls who are brave enough to do this, you can get the oldest person around to kick the wolf and say:

> *Go, fly, away to the sky.*
> *Devilish graywolf, we do thee defy.*
> *Out, out, out, with a howl and a yell*
> *That will carry you faster and surer to hell.*

And if you can't find an old person who is willing to do this, you can gather a crowd of people and have everyone throw a hot mixture of sulphur, tea, vinegar, and castoreum at the creature, all the while shouting at the werewolf to go away.

Finally, if you believe that werewolfism is something inside the body that can be gotten out with laxatives and things that will bring on vomiting, do this:

Open a vein and cause the blood to drain until the animal faints. Then feed the creature and bathe it. Sprinkle it with whey (the liquid you get when you curdle milk) for three days and feed it food that will cause it to go to the bathroom a lot.

Then work at getting the evil out of the other end of its body. Give it things like aloe and wormwood and vinegar. If these things don't make it vomit, take stronger action. Make it drink hellebore. Rub its nostrils with opium. Once it throws up repeatedly, it will be cured.

Obviously, you had to care a great deal about the person trapped inside the werewolf's body to go through all this trouble. But if someone you cared about was a werewolf, you would be happy to do whatever you could to help.

Why didn't the authorities and judges and inquisitors try these things? The answer is that probably most of them didn't want to. Some of these judges really believed there was no cure for werewolves and that trying to work a cure would be like trying to do business with the devil.

Other judges believed that the only way to stop people from taking up with the devil was to show what horrible things happened to people who did. They didn't care what happened to those persons they made examples of.

Still others just liked the idea of having the power of life or death over other people and used that power happily.

But there was one local government in France over three hundred years ago that did care. It didn't try any cures on the werewolf convicted in its area; but it decided that no purpose would be served by executing him. This is what happened.

In 1603 in a village in the southwest of France, a young teenage boy named Jean Grenier began to boast about being a werewolf. He told three girls that a man had given him a wolfskin cape and that the man wrapped it around him every Monday, Friday, and Sunday. For about an hour at dusk each day, he became a werewolf.

The girls immediately reported the boy to the authorities. And since several children had been killed in the area recently, Jean Grenier was arrested.

By this time there were many people in France who were not very proud of all the executions of witches and werewolves that had taken place over the last century. No longer were the courts inclined to believe every witness and every bit of circumstantial evidence. The court officers spent a lot of time checking on the evidence. But Jean Grenier kept insisting that he was a werewolf and that he had indeed killed the children who had died in the area. The court ruled that he should be hanged and his body burned to ashes.

But a higher court decided to review the case. After hearing the youth's confession, the Parlement of Bordeaux was still not satisfied. The members decided to look into the boy's family background and found tragedy. They voted to send two doctors to examine Jean Grenier. The doctors reported that the boy was suffering from the disease of lycanthropy. They didn't give a scientific explanation. They said an evil spirit had caused the disease. But they did say that Jean Grenier had only *imagined* he turned into a wolf.

The Parlement of Bordeaux chose to believe the doctors and to take into account what they had found out about Jean Grenier's background. Its ruling is remarkable for its intelligence in a day when people still believed that the devil was as powerful as God. Here is part of its opinion:

> *The court, in conclusion, takes into account the young age and imbecility of this boy, who is so stupid and idiotic that children of seven and eight years old normally show more intelligence, who has been ill fed in every respect and who is so dwarfed that he is not as tall as a ten-year-old. . . . Here is a young lad abandoned and driven out by his father, who has a cruel stepmother instead of a real mother, who wanders over the fields, without a counselor and without anyone to take an interest in him, begging his bread, who has never had any religious training, whose real nature was corrupted by evil promptings, need, and despair, and whom the devil made his prey.*

The Parlement of Bordeaux overruled the lower court and changed Jean Grenier's sentence to life imprisonment in a local monastery.

It would be nice to say that Jean Grenier got better after that. But he was sick, and being in the monastery didn't help him very much. He died in 1610, when he was about twenty-one years old. The Franciscan monks at the monastery said he died "as a good Christian," but a man who visited him in the year he died reported that Jean still believed he had been a werewolf and still thought he would like to eat children, if he could.

It is certainly odd that Jean Grenier, one of the few accused werewolves in history not to have been executed, died young anyway. Perhaps it is even more odd, and says something ironic about life, that of all people he was allowed to live out his natural life while so many others who never even imagined being werewolves and who confessed to being werewolves only because they couldn't stand being tortured any longer, died horribly and wrongfully.

CHAPTER XXII
THE MYTHS PERSIST

The best werewolf cure of all was knowledge. The more you know, the less likely you are to be frightened.

By the 1600s, advances in human knowledge were helping to change the way people looked at the world around them and to make them less afraid. These advances included Galileo's experiments with gravity, Copernicus's theories about the nature of the universe (especially that the earth and the other planets revolved around the sun, not viceversa), Mercator's formula for making maps of a round world instead of a flat one, the invention of the printing press, and some discoveries in medicine showing that many diseases were not caused by evil spirits.

By the 1600s, both the Church and ordinary people were beginning to have a different attitude toward werewolves. They were not so quick to believe in animal demons and were more likely to see that people who believed themselves to be werewolves were just insane. Courts were not so quick to believe circumstantial evidence. In other words, you were no longer automatically thought to be a werewolf just because your eyebrows met across the top of your nose or because you happened to be in a place where a wolf had just been.

But there continued to be many incidents involving suspected werewolves. In fact, the belief in werewolves continues even to this day in some areas.

The more rural areas of Italy are an example. In the Alpine provinces, people still think of a stream near Cimapiasole as a magic body of water where werewolves go to drink in order to change into animal form. In another area, people still put wax crosses on their doors at Christmastime to keep werewolves away.

In Palermo, people say that as the moon starts to become full the werewolf (in human form) has muscle spasms and finally writhes on the ground in pain. At that point, he or she turns into a wolf and, howling, rushes off on all fours and will attack anyone or any animal found. The werewolf may even try to break into his or her own house. But if experienced, the werewolf will have warned family members to lock all the doors and windows and at daybreak he or she will automatically go back into human form.

On July 5, 1949, the London *Daily Telegraph* carried this report from its correspondent in Rome: "Howls coming from the bushes in gardens in the centre of Rome last night brought a police patrol to what seemed a 'werewolf.' Under the full moon they found a young man, Pasquale Rosini, covered in mud, digging in the ground with his finger-nails and howling. On being taken to the hospital Rosini said that for three years he had regularly lost consciousness at periods of the full moon and had found himself wandering the streets at night, driven by uncontrollable instincts. He was sent to a clinic for observation."

The werewolf myth seems to be alive in France, too. A French expert on folklore named Claude Seignolle wrote about a case that was supposed to have taken place around the turn of the century. A French farmer out walking in the woods saw two wolves. Afraid they might attack him, he climbed a tree. But they had not seen him, and they stopped practically right under the tree. To the farmer's amazement, they started to talk to one another in human voices. Not only that, but one of them took a snuff box from under its tail and offered some of the tobacco to the other. After a while they left.

The farmer climbed down from the tree and saw that the wolves had dropped the snuff box. He took it with him and was able to trace it to a man who lived nearby. Although the farmer often told the story of how he had spied on two werewolves, he never revealed their names until one of them died. Every morning the dead man's gravestone showed fresh scratches, as if it had been clawed by an animal. The farmer explained that this was because the man had been a werewolf.

In November 1925 there was a curious case in the Alsace region of France. The policeman of a small village near Strasbourg was arrested and tried for shooting and killing a boy. In his defense the policeman said that he had long been haunted by animals with human faces. The boy knew this and had played tricks on him. But, he said, this was no ordinary mischief. The boy had, through sorcery, gained the power to turn himself into a wolf. The village people believed the policeman.

In the winter of 1930 in Bourg-la-Reine in France, a farmer named Richard disappeared. His neighbors were glad he was gone because he had a reputation as a sorcerer and was believed to "walk by night in the shape of a wolf." In his cabin were found herbs, charms, and magic stones, a calf's head, and wax dolls labeled with the names of people in the neighborhood—all of whom had died. One doll was labeled with the name of an important landowner, and there was a pin stuck through its throat. The landowner had died of cancer of the throat.

In North America, Navajo Indian folklore includes stories about werewolves and were-bears meeting at night and moving so fast that no one could catch them, but leaving tracks in the shape of paws. Lying in their hogans at night, the Navajos would tremble with fear when they heard the creatures outside. Alberta Hannum wrote about the Navajo belief in werewolves in a book published in 1947 called *Spin a Silver Dollar*: "Sometimes the wolf would knock four times, or sometimes the people inside the hogan would only hear the mud falling from the roof and know it was the wolf there. But always, with or without warning, the wolf appeared with paralyzing slowness to its victims—peeping around the corner of the door blanket, or letting just its eyes show for a while over the hole in the roof, and then slowly the rest of him."

The Navajos believed werewolves caused tuberculosis, a disease that used to kill many Indians every year. A wolf would throw a powder down on the hogan fire and make it flare and stink, and the evil fumes would get into their lungs.

In the 1940s in Arizona, a group of Navajos believed that a werewolf lived among them. In fact they called the suspected man "The Werewolf." They believed he turned himself into a wolf at night and raided their flocks of sheep and that he dug up graves and robbed the corpses of their jewels. But the worst fear people had about him was that in his nightly wolf form he also killed and ate people, usually women.

It was reliably reported that the man did sometimes dress himself up in animal skins at night and go out and attack women. He also apparently had a suspiciously large number of sheep and a great amount of silver and jewelry.

The image of the wolf as a stealthy creature who hunts its victims down in the dead of night is very much alive in our minds today. In Germany between the two World Wars there was a group that called themselves the "Werewolf Organization." It was a secret terrorist organization founded in 1923 on the model of the Sicilian Mafia and dedicated to political assassination. After World War II it was started up again as an underground resistance movement and was responsible for the murders of several anti-Nazi German officials as well as a number of soldiers in the French occupation army. In

May 1946 a London newspaper carried the report that the "secret" grave of the Italian dictator Benito Mussolini had been decorated with a wreath that bore the inscription "We shall avenge you. The wolves are awaiting their chance to spring."

And finally, there are still enough reports of strange creatures to keep us guessing. In Pakistan in August 1966 there were reports that an awful monster was terrorizing the people of Jesore in the eastern part of the country. According to the Associated Press, the monster had gone on a series of nighttime raids, killing a baby, attacking and mauling several other people, and killing many cattle. Every time the police or armed citizens set out after it, the beast vanished. At length it disappeared for good, leaving behind no clue to its identity.

We cannot say for sure what kind of beast terrorized Jesore. But something killed those cattle and that infant and attacked those people.

Every now and then there are reports from other parts of the world about huge creatures that seem to be half human and half animal. Have you ever heard of Big Foot or the Abominable Snowman?

Most people today do not believe in werewolves or wereanythings. But as long as people think of the wolf when they think of treachery and stealth, and as long as there are unexplained happenings such as the one at Jesore, the myth of the man-animal, and the myth of the werewolf, will stay alive.

SOME OTHER BOOKS ABOUT WEREWOLVES

Aylesworth, Thomas G. *The Story of Werewolves.* New York: McGraw-Hill, 1978

Baring-Gould, Sabine. *The Book of Werewolves.* New York: Causeway Books, 1973

Hill, Douglas, and Pat Williams. *The Supernatural.* New York: Hawthorn Books, 1965

McHargue, Georgess. *Meet the Werewolf.* Philadelphia and New York: J. B. Lippincott, 1976

Newton, Michael. *Monsters, Mysteries and Man.* Reading, Mass.: Addison-Wesley, 1979

Robbins, Rossell Hope. *The Encyclopedia of Witchcraft and Demonology.* New York: Crown Publishers, 1959

Summers, Montague. *Geography of Witchcraft.* London: Routledge & Kegan, 1978. Repr. of 1927 ed.

———. *The Werewolf.* New Hyde Park, New York: University Books, 1966

INDEX

Aesop's fables, 10
Abominable Snowman, the, 110
Africa, 2–3, 17
Alaska, 13
Albania, 13
All Saints Day, 72
Alsace region, France, 108
Altona (Hamburg), Germany, 53
Anthos race, 16
Arcadia region, Greece, 16
Arizona, 109
Ascension Day, 90
Asia, 13
Auvergne, France, 58

Babylon, 89
Bathory, Elizabeth, 4
Berserkers, 17
Bible, the, 11
Big Foot, 110

Bourg-la-Reine, France, 108
Bourgot, Pierre, 71–72
Britain
    werewolf beliefs in, 10, 13, 88, 90
    werewolf stories from, 35–36, 94
    witch trials in, 89
Brittany region, France, 58–59
Bulgaria, 13

Calmar Province, Sweden, 40
Canary Islands, 23
Chastel, Jean, 31, 33
China, 2, 18–19
Christianity, 3, 71–72, 89–90
Christmas, 22, 40, 42, 77, 88, 107
Cimapiasole, Italy, 107
Cologne, Germany, 68
Cumberland County, England, 35

D'Apcher, Marquis, 31
Demons, 63, 65, 79, 88, 90
Denmark, 99
De Poiret, Rimbaud, 58
Devil, the, 10, 53–54, 69, 71–73, 94, 99, 102–103
    pacts with, 53–54, 68, 78, 81
Dionysius, 16
Dole, France, 72
Duhamel, Captain Jacques, 31

Eastern Europe, 47–48. See also Poland; Russia; and other countries
Eisler, Dr. Robert, 23–24
Ericksburg, Germany, 55
Eurasia, 13
Europe, 4, 11, 13, 15, 17–18, 23, 63, 65–66. See also Britain; France; and other countries
Exorcism, 100

Films, 2, 4, 76, 90, 94, 97
Finland, 13, 40
France
    werewolf beliefs in, 3, 77, 81, 107–108
    werewolf stories from, 30–31, 33, 58–60, 90–91, 100
    werewolf and witch trials in, 65, 71–73, 102–103
    wolves in, 13

Gandillon family, 73

Garnier, Gilles, 72
Germany, 18
    werewolf beliefs in, 3, 81, 90, 99–100, 109
    werewolf stories from, 53–56
    werewolf and witch trials in, 4, 65, 68
Gonzales, Peter, 23
Greece, 18
    proverbs from, 10–11
    werewolf beliefs in, 100
    werewolf stories from, 15–16, 19
Grenier, Jean, 102–103
Gypsies, 47

Hamburg, Germany, 53–54
Hannum, Alberta, 109
Hesse, Germany, 54
Hindenburg, Germany, 55
Hitler, Adolf, 18
Hungary, 3–4, 47–48
Hydrophobia. See Rabies
Hypertrichosis, 23–24

Iceland, 81
India, 2
Indians (North American,) 3–4, 108–109
Inquisition, the, 64–65
Ireland
    werewolf beliefs in, 10, 26, 42, 80, 100
    werewolf stories from, 26–27
Irish wolfhound, 13, 26
Isawiyya brotherhood, 17

Italy, 18
    werewolf beliefs in, 10, 16–17, 77, 89–90, 100, 107
    werewolf stories from, 22, 50–51, 100
    wolves in, 13

Jesore, Pakistan, 110

King Henry II, 23
King John, 35
King Louis XV, 31

Latin America, 2–3
Le Gévaudan, France, 30–31
Le Sorge d'Auvert, France, 33
Little Red Riding Hood, 11
Lone Ranger, the, 94
Lycanthropy, 21–22, 73, 103
Lycaon, 15–16

Maenad tribe, 16
Man into Wolf, 23
Man-animals, 2–3, 17, 35, 108
Matthew, Book of, 11
Meath, Ireland, 27
Merionethshire, Wales, 36
Middle East, 18
Morocco, 17
Moscow, 22
Mt. Lycaeus (Mt. St. Elias), 16
Mt. Olympus, 15
Mussolini, Benito, 110

Navajo Indians, 108–109
Normans, 35, 38

Norway, 80

O'Donnell, Elliott, 35
Ossory district, Ireland, 26

Pakistan, 110
Palermo, Italy, 50–51, 107
Parlement of Bordeaux, 102–103
Pliny, 10
Poitiers, France, 59
Poland, 28, 42–44, 47
Poligny district, France, 71
Pope Innocent III, 64
Pope John XXIV, 65
Porphyria, 22–23
Portefaix, Andre, 31
Portugal, 27
Pourcher, Jean-Pierre, 30
Protestant Church, 63, 65
Prussia, 48
Puritans, 65

Quedlinburg, Germany, 65

Rabies, 85, 89
Robbins, Rossell, 65
Roman Catholic Church, 63–65, 106
Rome, Italy, 64, 107
Rosini, Pasquale, 107
Rumania, 47
Russia
    werewolf beliefs in, 47, 80–81, 94
    werewolf stories from, 22, 40
    wolves in, 13

St. Claude, France, 73
Saint Etienne de Lugardes, France, 30
St. John's Day, 22, 42, 77
Salaparuta, Italy, 50
Salem, Massachusetts, 65, 89
Saxony region, Germany, 65
Scandinavia
    werewolf beliefs in, 77, 81, 83
    werewolf stories from, 38, 40
    wolves in, 12
    See also Finland; Norway; and other countries
Scotland, 94
Seignolle, Claude, 107
Serbia, 3
Shansi Province, China, 19
She Wolf of London, 1946, 4
She-wolves. See Werewolves, female
Shepherd and the Wolf, The, 10
Sicily, 10, 13, 17
Sigmund the Volsung, 38
Slavic countries, 47. See also Poland; Rumania; and other countries
Sorcery, 10, 65, 77–78, 89, 108. See also Witchcraft
Spin a Silver Dollar, 109
Steena, Germany, 55
Strasbourg, France, 108
Stump (Stubb), Peter, 4, 68–69, 81

Sweden
    werewolf beliefs in, 80
    werewolf stories from, 40
    wolves in, 13

Three Little Pigs, The, 11
Tórész, Hungary, 47–48
Transylvania, 47

Ulster, Ireland, 26–27

Vampires, 3, 35, 47, 79, 88, 90, 94
Verdun, Michel, 71–72
Versailles, France, 31, 33
Vistula River, 43

Wales, 36
Werewolf, The, 1913, 4
"Werewolf Organization, The," 109–110
Werewolves
    characteristics of, 47, 64, 83, 85–86
    definition of, 2–3
    female, 4, 19, 27, 48, 54–55, 80
Witchcraft, 2, 63–65, 73, 89
Witches, 3, 10, 42–43, 47, 59, 63, 65–66, 72–73, 77–78, 93, 102
Wolf and the Crane, The, 11
"Wolfman Jack," 83
Wolves, 6, 9–11, 13, 15–16, 18–19, 43, 48, 109

Yugoslavia, 13

Zeus Lycaeus, 16